Lecture Notes
in Economics and
Mathematical Systems

Managing Editors: M. Beckmann and W. Krelle

289

Bert R. Meijboom

Planning in Decentralized Firms

A Contribution to the Theory
on Multilevel Decisions

Springer-Verlag
Berlin Heidelberg New York London Paris Tokyo

Managing Editors

Prof. Dr. M. Beckmann
Brown University
Providence, RI 02912, USA

Prof. Dr. W. Krelle
Institut für Gesellschafts- und Wirtschaftswissenschaften
der Universität Bonn
Adenauerallee 24–42, D-5300 Bonn, FRG

Author

Dr. Bert R. Meijboom
AKB, Consultants for Management Science and Software Development
P.O.Box 20720, NL-3014 DA Rotterdam, The Netherlands

ISBN 3-540-17795-7 Springer-Verlag Berlin Heidelberg New York
ISBN 0-387-17795-7 Springer-Verlag New York Berlin Heidelberg

aan Pap, Mam en Hedy
aan Jacqueline

<u>Preface</u>

The completion of this thesis gives me feelings of satisfaction and thankfulness. Satisfaction because its results appear to be worthwile and relevant, and thankfulness towards so many persons who contributed to the progress of the work.

The project "Analysis of multilevel decisions" was granted by the common research pool of Tilburg University and Eindhoven University of Technology (Samenwerkingsorgaan Brabantse Universiteiten). During the 4-year leadtime, the Department of Econometrics of Tilburg University provided not only a single room but also a pleasant and inspiring environment, for which I am very grateful.

The research itself, particularly the inevitable scientific struggles, was perfectly coached by my promotors, Prof. Dr. P.A. Verheyen and Prof. Dr. J.F. Benders. I cannot give even the slightest description of the unique way in which they managed to do this. In all criticism they succeeded to maintain a positive, and thus stimulating, working atmosphere.

The work also benefited from the suggestions given by Prof. Dr. Th.M.A. Bemelmans, Prof. Dr. J.P.C. Kleijnen, Prof. Dr. P.H.M. Ruys and Prof. Dr. A. Schrijver. Furthermore I am indebted to Dr. Adam Woźniak (Warsaw University of Technology), who made me participate in his multilevel experience and critically commented on an earlier draft of the thesis.

Through the years I enjoyed the support of several internal services of Tilburg University. Especially I wish to mention the typing staff of the Faculty of Economics. Mrs. Petra Ligtenberg typed the present text in a most efficient way keeping cool under the author's ever increasing nervous behaviour. Mr. Jan Pijnenburg assisted in completing the tables and figures, and Mr. Frans Buskens made the design for the front cover. Mrs. Hildegard Penn substantially improved the English text.

Finally I wish to thank all colleagues, friends and relatives for en-
couragement, enthusiasm and, last but not least, friendship.

January 1987

Bert Meijboom

<u>Contents</u>

CHAPTER ONE

INTRODUCTION

1.1. Problem statement

This thesis deals with the problem of multilevel decision-making. To be more specific, the planning process in a general, two-level, decentralized enterprise is investigated.

In big companies processes of specialization and differentiation usually lead to a decentralized organization structure with two or more hierarchical levels. A number of product divisions and service departments is present and the information on the basis of which decisions must be made is dispersed among these subunits. Due to the delegation of tasks and responsibilities, managers at several levels in the organization become local decision-makers, possibly with individual goals and preferences.

In order to realize the objectives of the company as a whole, the top management has to coordinate the managers of the subunits. The parts of the organization must be in balance. For instance, the way in which the top management allocates resources, directly ('budgets') or through an internal price system ('transfer prices'), should guide local decision-makers in choosing actions that are desired for the company as a whole.

It is clear that under such circumstances the decision-making process is not simple. Decisions cannot be made at once, but are usually preceeded by a phase of preparations, negotiations, information gathering etc. This phase will be referred to as the 'planning phase'. It ends as soon as the ultimate plan to be carried out is established. At this point the execution phase starts, in which actions are taken according to the decisions made upon termination of the planning phase. Possibly some form of evaluation or control is then desired to check whether actions have been carried out correctly.

We will focus on the information dispersal being one of the essential dimensions of the issue of decentralization in the enterprise, and investigate how the top management determines the decisions to be carried out without having complete information. Furthermore the analysis as provided in this book concentrates on the planning phase. The problem the top management is faced with during the planning phase will be called the planning problem. As a third preliminary, we consider a situation with only two hierarchical levels. Due to the localized information, the interaction between the two levels is a matter of information exchange.

This introductory problem description shows the practical relevance of the topic. However, the approach to be presented is a theoretical one. Concepts from three theoretical areas, namely the theory of the firm, management accounting and organization theory will be combined in building the model of a general, two-level, decentralized firm. We follow the activity analysis approach for the representation of the prevalent production possibilities to be chosen from by the management of the firm. A second realistic feature is the incorporation of cost allocation mechanisms, as frequently advocated in accounting literature. Thirdly, issues such as decentralization, delegation and coordination will be accounted for because of our interest in multilevel decisions.

Having outlined the main characteristics of the object of our study, i.e. a general two-level enterprise, we turn to the methodological aspects. As an abstraction of reality we will use formal models. This means that our analysis is based on a mathematical representation of the planning problem at hand. Furthermore mathematical techniques will be introduced that function as conceptual tools in developing a planning model and particularly not as computational methods or as solution algorithms. Thus we aim at building a conceptual framework for planning in decentralized organizations: a planning model. The model formulation will be deterministic and static because we ignore uncertainty and time-dependent aspects.

From the large field of multilevel systems analysis we apply the theory on decomposition for large-scale linear programming problems. The linearity of problem formulations is not really restrictive in the present descriptive study. The decomposition approach is suitable for planning with incomplete information at the top level of the organization. It should be noted that we presume a form of harmony between the top management and the lower level managers. Because of agreement on the objectives for the firm as a whole, each one is willing to participate in the planning process. There is no conflict of interests. As a consequence we can (and will) use optimization models with a one-dimensional objective function.

The book concludes with an application of the decomposition philosophy to the model of the firm. After having built this model we will also analyse and solve the associated planning problem.

The aim of this book is threefold:

First of all, a general model of the firm is to be designed. By 'general' we mean that the model takes into account technological, financial and organizational issues as prevalent in real-world enterprises. Through the process of developing the model we will demonstrate the relevance of analysing multilevel decisions. Furthermore the model will serve as the basic framework when we investigate the two-level planning process.

The second goal of the book is of a methodological nature, namely to analyse planning in a two-level organization from a formal and an abstract point of view. To this end two elementary decomposition-based planning procedures will be reviewed to illustrate the conceptual usefulness of decomposition techniques. One typical feature is that in a similar procedure coordination is accomplished by prices or by direct allocations, analogous to price and budget directive planning in existing organizations. Moreover we will present a new decomposition technique in which prices and direct allocations occur simultaneously.

The third goal is to compare 'overall modelling' with 'multilevel modelling'. More specifically, we will describe how the planning problem of our fictitious firm would be solved in the case of complete information and in the case of decentralized information. We also compare the requirements for cost allocations under both types of circumstances. Concretely this means that, apart from solving the planning problem directly, we also apply a decomposition-based planning procedure. We then analyse the flow of information during the planning process and incorporate cost allocation mechanisms in the procedure.

In effect, the present book contributes to the theory on multilevel
decisions because
- a new mixed price-resource directive decomposition will be presented;
- the effect of decomposition-based planning is analysed in the context
  of an input-output inspired model of the firm.
As our model of the firm captures a number of realistic features, the
final part of the book may contribute to the understanding of two-level
planning as observed in the real-world.

1.2. <u>Outline of the book</u>

The body of the book is organized according to the three goals as set
out above.

In chapter two the technological part of our general model of the firm,
i.e. the corporate model, is developed. The production transformation
processes are described in terms of an input-output model of the firm.
However, the element of choice, e.g. decisions concerning alternative
production techniques, cannot be represented by such a model. Therefore
we generalize the input-output model by introducing multiple techniques
and make-or-buy decisions. We end with a mixed-integer programming model
that integrates all alternatives to be decided upon into one overall
formulation.

Chapter three extends the corporate model with financial and organizational features. Being an important financial aspect, the issue of cost
allocation is discussed. After some definitions and examples we explain
why cost allocation is a most realistic option to be included in our
model, especially in the context of multilevel decision-making. Then we
propose the organizational structure for our hypothetical firm. The corporate model will be reformulated in such a way that it reflects the
assumed divisional organization structure.

In chapter four we start analysing two-level planning with incomplete
information at the higher level in the organization. Under these circumstances it is appropriate to apply decomposition-based planning procedures. The subunits at the lower level in the organization are usually

coordinated indirectly, by prices, or directly, by resource allocations. As an example of price-directive planning we discuss the famous method of Dantzig-Wolfe. Similarly, Benders' method is treated, being a well-known resource-directive approach. For completeness the mathematical derivation is provided in an appendix.

In existing organizations, however, indirect and direct coordination instruments may well occur simultaneously. In chapter five we analyse such settings formally by describing mixed price-resource directive planning procedures. The formal derivation of the presented procedures is integrated in the text because the underlying mathematics are scarcely touched in the literature.

Having investigated the planning problem from a rather abstract, conceptual point of view, we return to our general, two-level, divisionalized enterprise as developed in chapters two and three. In chapter six the planning problem as stated at the end of chapter three is analysed under the assumption of complete information. The top management is supposed to have a complete specification of all relevant data. Hence the planning problem can be solved without the participation of managers of sub-units. This overall approach thus ignores organizational aspects and provides some provisional but limited insight into the firm under consideration.

Of course, the assumption of complete information is quite unrealistic, especially at the presumed organizational conditions. In order to account for the divisionalization and the information dispersal, we apply the decomposition philosophy as introduced in chapters four and five. Before actually solving the planning problem, the top management has to gather information. The data as exchanged between the two organizational levels will appear to be of an aggregated nature. Tentative, intermediate solutions can differ essentially from the ultimate, firm-wide optimal solution. Cost allocation mechanisms should be incorporated very carefully.

We construct a numerical example which is used in chapters six and seven in order to illustrate our results in an informal way.

Now the three goals of the book are achieved and we review and evaluate the research in the final chapter.

1.3. <u>Relevant economic literature</u>

The present study is a theoretical one. It integrates elements and concepts from a number of economic and mathematical theories. In the remainder of this introductory chapter these theories are briefly reviewed. We present a short description of some relevant contributions and point out opportunities for extension of existing theories. We start with economics. In the next section, key references concerning multi-level systems analysis are given.

First of all the theory of the firm. Naylor and Vernon (1969, p. 2) stated that "what is designated in economics as 'the economic theory of the firm' is a collection of theories about the behavior of firms operating under a very special set of environmental conditions known in the aggregate as a market economy". One indispensable element in theoretical models of firms is the notion of a production transformation process. Basically, two approaches in describing the production transformation process can be distinguished: marginal analysis and activity (or programming) analysis. Compare chapter eleven and twelve in Baumol (1977). The latter approach is felt to be more realistic and will be adopted here.

A typical restriction of the theory of the firm is that the firm is viewed as an entity directed by or identified with a single decision-maker, the entrepreneur. In other words, the organizational structure and its impact on decision-making are not considered.

In the literature on management and organizations issues like decentralization, delegation and coordination are discussed based on the observation that today's business enterprises are often very large and thus face complex problems. See Dessler (1982, ch. 7), Dopuch et al. (1982, ch. 10), Kaplan (1982, ch. 13). An interesting and useful attempt to build a conceptual framework concerning decentralization in organizations can be found in Jennergren (1980). He states that "decentralization usually refers to the hierarchical levels on which decisions are made" (p. 39) and that "delegation is sometimes used interchangeably with decentralization. However, often it has a more concrete meaning, implying a specification of the tasks delegated or persons to whom decision-making authority is assigned" (p. 41). Furthermore it is explained how decentralization in firms leads to certain organizational forms. The components of the organization, product divisions and functional departments, must then be coordinated.

Coordination instruments can be price-directive or resource-directive. In an almost classical paper Hirschleifer (1956) stated that "the problem of pricing the goods and services that are exchanged between divisions within a firm (...) is an important one, because prices which are set on internal transfers affect the level of activity within divisions (...) and the total profit that is achieved by the firm as a whole". Hence it is clear that such transfer prices can be used to coordinate subunits in the firm.

On the other hand, budgets can be applied for coordination, too. In Dopuch et al. (1982, p. 199) a budget is described as a "formal, quantitative statement of anticipated resource flows". Anthony and Dearden (1976, p. 20) speak of an "approved statement of the revenues that are expected during the budget year, and the resources that are to be used in achieving the company's goals for each responsibility center and for the company as a whole". Thus budgets are resource-directive coordination instruments.

It should be mentioned that we ignore another well-known function of transfer prices and budgets, namely performance evaluation.

In textbooks on management accounting very much attention is paid to transfer pricing and budgeting. We refer to Kaplan (1982, ch. 14,17). Moreover, Kaplan (1982, p. 5) formulates "an empirical question, to which we do not have an answer, as to why companies continue to use fully allocated costs for internal decision and control purposes". Indeed, in the recent literature there is a growing interest in cost allocation and its role in decision-making processes (see e.g. Biddle and Steinberg (1985)) so that ideas from this field must be considered.

1.4. <u>The multilevel approach</u>

As the final section of this chapter, we present important contributions concerning the basic concept or philosophy applied in this book, i.e.

the literature on multilevel decision-making. Firstly, we will clarify
the term 'multilevel'.

Dirickx and Jennergren (1979, p. 2) state that "in the multilevel
methods of modeling and solving a decision problem, a complete representation is put together from subproblems, where each subproblem refers to
some part of the whole problem situation. (...) The subproblems form an
interrelated hierarchy, which means that they are considered to be on
different hierarchical levels". Furthermore, "the subproblems must be
coordinated in some fashion, and one function of higher-level subproblems is to coordinate the lower-level ones".

As one of the most important contributions to the theory of multilevel
decision-making, we mention Mesarović et al. (1970). In this book the
relevance of multilevel systems to organization theory is argued,
notions such as 'hierarchy' and 'multilevel' are discussed and formalized, and a mathematical theory of coordination is developed. In a later
paper Jennergren (1976) advocates a broader framework for what he calls
'the multilevel approach'. In his point of view, material as presented
by Mesarović et al. (and thus also the later work by Findeisen et al.
(1980)) are typically highly formalized approaches for solving problems
in a multilevel fashion.

The common feature in these contributions is the occurrence of decomposition, i.e. to break up a big problem into small ones and to try to
coordinate the small problems so that they together yield a solution to
the big one. In this way a large variety of computational, technological, economical and social problems can, in principle, be tackled. So
the multilevel approach implies a way of modelling and solving problems
in which one is forced to (try to) identify subcomponents and their in-
terrelationships.

Decomposition-based planning procedures will be applied here as conceptual tools for analysing two-level planning problems in companies. A
recent, useful reference in this area is Obel (1981), who introduced
mixed price-resource directive decomposition methods.

CHAPTER TWO

THE MODEL OF THE FIRM:
MULTIPLE TECHNIQUES AND MAKE-OR-BUY DECISIONS

2.1. Introduction

This chapter and the next are devoted to the design of a general model
of the firm. In the present chapter the technological part of the model,
to be referred to as the corporate model, is considered. The well-known
input-output model of the firm is taken as a starting point for the presentation of the corporate model.

Originally introduced in macroeconomics by Leontief (1936), input-output analysis has become a widespread and fruitful approach in corporate
modelling as well (Livingstone (1969), Verheyen (1965)). Input-output
models can be applied in practice, e.g. in planning and budgeting (see
Horngren (1982, ch. 14), Kaplan (1982, ch. 11)). Besides they are useful
in more theoretical areas, in particular in the activity analysis
approach for the multiproduct firm (see Knudsen (1973, ch. 5), Naylor
and Vernon (1969, ch. 8)).

After a first rough sketch of the corporate model, expressed in common
input-output terminology (section 2.2), the basic model is generalized,
by the allowance for multiple techniques (section 2.3) and make-or-buy
decisions (section 2.4).

2.2. The firm in input-output terminology

We consider a firm producing the following three types of commodities:
market products, technical services (TS) and general services (GS). The
sector 'market products' yields the actual output of the firm, the final
output. We assume that this sector incurs variable costs only. Furthermore, its activities require certain technical services (e.g. housekee-
ping, data processing, maintenance, catering). Production of technical
services leads to variable and fixed costs. Finally, there is a sector

producing certain general services (e.g. research and development, public relations, corporate management). In this sector, only fixed costs,
the so-called common costs, are incurred.

Output from one sector may be input elsewhere in the firm, and input
factors exist which come from outside the firm, the so-called primary
input, like labour and raw materials. All these deliveries and transactions can be taken together in the well-known input-output table (see
figure 2.1).

To From	general services	technical services	market products	final output
general services				✕
technical services				✕
market products				
primary input				✕

Figure 2.1: General input-output table; only 'market products' delivers
to 'final output'. A cross expresses the absence of certain
deliveries.

In common input-output analysis (e.g. Livingstone (1969), Smits and
Verheyen (1976), Verheyen (1965)), it is assumed that
- there is a constant final demand for market products,
- the market prices for primary input are constants,
- a transfer-price scheme for internal deliveries and an allocation
  scheme for common costs have been established,
- the production of every commodity obeys a linear homogeneous production function (constant returns to scale).
Based on the knowledge of final demand and production function, an input-output table on a real basis (quantities of products and services)

can be drawn. Using the prices for primary input, the transfer prices for internal deliveries and the allocation scheme for common costs, the table can be transformed into an input-output table on a nominal basis, (all transactions expressed in monetary terms). Although the actual input-output relations are approximated, by assuming a linear production function, the approach may well yield satisfactory computational results, e.g. for cost accounting purposes.

After this rather informal outline of the corporate model, we continue with the formalization of the input-output model of the firm. For the purpose of the present chapter, the GS sector does not need to be taken into consideration, yet.

There are M types of technical services and Φ types of market products, denoted by $TS_1,\ldots,TS_m,\ldots,TS_M$ and $X_1,\ldots,X_\phi,\ldots,X_\Phi$ respectively. Focusing on the internal deliveries within the firm, we consider an input-output table where the sectors 'primary input' and 'final output' are omitted: see figure 2.2. Every D^{flow} matrix represents the deliveries between and within sectors, expressed in physical quantities. For instance $D^{flow}_{M\Phi}$ is an M x Φ matrix whose (m,ϕ)-th element $D^{flow}_{m\phi}$ represents the flow of commodities from TS_m to X_ϕ .

From \ To	$TS_1 \cdots TS_M$	$X_1 \cdots X_\Phi$
TS_1 $\vdots$ TS_M	D^{flow}_{MM}	$D^{flow}_{M\Phi}$
X_1 $\vdots$ X_Φ		$D^{flow}_{\Phi\Phi}$

Figure 2.2:   Input-output table for corporate model, the sectors 'primary input' and 'final output' deleted.

It is assumed that every input is a linear homogeneous function of the output. For each of the products and services, fixed ratios exist between input and output. E.g. we have

$$D_{m\phi}^{flow} = D_{m\phi} x(\phi), \qquad\qquad (2.1)$$

where $x(\phi) \geqslant 0$ denotes the production volume of product X_ϕ. The constant coefficient $D_{m\phi}$ is called an <u>intermediate input coefficient</u>. We require $D_{m\phi} \geqslant 0$. Similar formulas hold for the other D^{flow} matrices.

In this book, we will mainly use the intermediate input coefficients as just defined. Therefore we replace every element of D_{MM}^{flow}, $D_{M\phi}^{flow}$, $D_{\phi\phi}^{flow}$ by its corresponding intermediate input coefficient and call the obtained matrices D_{MM}, $D_{M\phi}$, $D_{\phi\phi}$ respectively.

Because of the linear production function, formulas like (2.1) can also be stated with respect to primary inputs. The associated coefficients are then primary input coefficients. The market for primary input is such that the firm can buy as much as it wants at fixed per-unit prices. Using the market prices for primary inputs, the costs of producing one unit of a product or service are easily found. These <u>per-unit direct cost coefficients</u> will be applied in our model formulation rather than the primary input coefficients.

Now we introduce two realistic features to be incorporated in the model. In input-output analysis each commodity requires input factors in fixed proportions. Or, stated differently, for each commodity exactly one linear production technique exists. In our model of the firm, however, it will be assumed that for each market product a choice can be made from a finite number of linear techniques. Market products of the same type but produced by different techniques are identical (and hence physically equivalent).

<u>Definition 2.1</u>:

A <u>technology alternative</u> is a collection of techniques, at least one for each product. A <u>pure</u> technology alternative applies exactly one technique per product.

As a second generalization of the input-output framework, we will account for the possibility that TS can also be bought externally, apart from being produced internally.

<u>Definition 2.2</u>:
A <u>TS alternative</u> is a combination of make-or-buy decisions stating which TS-types will be produced internally and which TS-types will be bought externally.

In the following sections, we will work out the two features and integrate all possible technology alternatives and TS alternatives in one overall model formulation.

2.3. <u>Multiple techniques for market products</u>

Because in reality the management of a firm usually can make a choice from a number of production possibilities, the notion of multiple techniques is further explored and incorporated in the corporate model. In this section, the TS sector is temporarily ignored, so that we can concentrate on the market products and their production process.

In the original input-output setting, the linearity assumption implies that each commodity requires inputs in fixed proportions. These fixed proportions follow from the input coefficients of that commodity, which, in turn, completely describe the production technique according to which that commodity is produced. In particular, for each market product exactly one production technique is supposed to be available.

In existing firms, however, input factors can often be combined in more than one way. In other words, multiple techniques for one specific market product can exist. Therefore we assume that for each market product X_ϕ a choice exists between Ψ_ϕ techniques. To this end we extend our corporate model as follows.

Originally, the ϕ-th column of matrix $D_{\phi\phi}$ plus the per-unit direct costs of market product X_ϕ formed a set of production coefficients that formally represented the, one and only, production technique for X_ϕ.

From now on, Ψ_ϕ sets of production coefficients are assumed to exist for X_ϕ. As before, each specific set of production coefficients consists of ϕ intermediate input coefficients and one per-unit direct cost coefficient. Being originally defined as the matrix of the (uniquely determined) intermediate input coefficients (see 2.2), $D_{\phi\phi}$ will, from now on, contain the intermediate input coefficients of each of the available techniques.

The occurrence of multiple techniques implies a certain degree of freedom for the management of the firm. Now the question arises which criterion is applied when choosing between alternatives. In the case of a fixed final output to be met, cost minimization will be the goal. If market restrictions exists that only pose a limit to the final output, the sales prices must be taken in account, so that profit maximization is a more appropriate objective. We will present the problem formulation for both situations. Firstly, some introductory definitions are in order.

Let $x_\phi(\psi)$ denote the units of produced X_ϕ by applying technique ψ ($\psi=1,\ldots,\Psi_\phi$). The production vector x_ϕ for market product X_ϕ is a column vector defined by $x_\phi := (x_\phi(1),\ldots,x_\phi(\Psi_\phi))'$ ($\phi=1,\ldots,\Phi$). The total production vector x_{prod} for the sector 'market products' is composed from these individual production vectors, i.e. $x_{prod} := (x_1',\ldots,x_\Phi')'$. Altogether:

total production $\qquad x_{prod} := (x_1',\ldots,x_\phi',\ldots,x_\Phi')'$

production vector
of product type X_ϕ $\qquad x_\phi' := (x_\phi(1),\ldots,x_\phi(\psi),\ldots,x_\phi(\psi_\phi))$

The corresponding per-unit direct costs $c_{M+\phi}(\psi)$ are taken together in the (row) vector c_{prod}, so

$$c_{prod} := (c_{M+1}(1),\ldots,c_{M+1}(\Psi_{M+1}),\ldots,c_{M+\phi}(1),\ldots,c_{M+\phi}(\Psi_{M+\phi}))$$

Because of the occurrence of more than one technique per market product, the new matrix $D_{\phi\phi}$ of intermediate input coefficients is not square.

Therefore, a 'generalized' identity matrix I_ϕ is required. More specifically, I_ϕ has the same dimensions as $D_{\phi\phi}$ and is of the form:

$$
I_\phi := \begin{bmatrix} 1\ldots1 & & \\ & \ddots & \\ & 1\ldots1 & \\ & & \ddots \\ & & 1\ldots1 \end{bmatrix} \updownarrow \phi
$$

$$
\underset{\Psi_1}{\longleftrightarrow} \quad \underset{\Psi_\phi}{\longleftrightarrow} \quad \underset{\Psi_\Phi}{\longleftrightarrow}
$$

The outside demand for X_ϕ is $f(\phi)$ $(\phi=1,\ldots,\Phi)$ and $f := (f(1),\ldots,f(\Phi))'$.
The technology alternative that can realize the final demand at minimal costs follows from the following linear programming (LP) problem:

$$
\begin{aligned}
\text{Minimize} \quad & c_{prod}\, x_{prod} \\
\text{s.t.} \quad & (I_\phi - D_{\phi\phi})\, x_{prod} = f \\
& x_{prod} \geqslant 0
\end{aligned}
\tag{2.2}
$$

The equality constraints express the relationship between production and outside supply of market products. The objective function equals the direct variable costs for primary input involved in the production process and is to be minimized. We require $c_{prod} > 0$, $f > 0$ and $D_{\phi\phi} \geqslant 0$.

Of course it would be convenient if a feasible solution exists to problem (2.2). This would imply the existence of an optimal solution, i.e. a cost minimizing technology alternative, because $c_{prod} > 0$.
If exactly one technique per product is available, matrix $I_\phi - D_{\phi\phi}$ is square and then a necessary and sufficient condition for feasibility of (2.2) is: $I_\phi - D_{\phi\phi}$ is invertible and $(I_\phi - D_{\phi\phi})^{-1} \geqslant 0$. In turn, this condition is equivalent to the usual input-output requirement: equation $(I_\phi - D_{\phi\phi})x = f$ has a non-negative solution for any $f \geqslant 0$.
We will not prove these conjectures. They are direct consequences of the theory of so-called M-matrices, that deals with generalizations of input-output matrices. We refer to Berman and Plemmons (1979, Ch. 6 and 9).

In the present situation, with $D_{\phi\phi}$ not square because of the occurrence of multiple techniques, the following result holds. We state a theorem that is proved in Appendix A.

<u>Theorem 2.1:</u>

Assume that problem (2.2) is feasible for a certain final demand vector f that is strictly positive. Now the following conjectures are true:

1. A cost minimizing technology alternative exists that can produce f while using exactly one technique per product. Moreover, this pure technology alternative can produce every non-negative final demand at minimal costs.

2. Let D^* be the square matrix of the intermediate input coefficients and let c^* be the row vector of the direct cost coefficients of the pure technology alternative at hand. Now:

   2.a. Matrix $(I-D^*)$ is invertible and $(I-D^*)^{-1} \geqslant 0$.

   2.b. $v^* := c^*(I-D^*)^{-1}$ is dual optimal.

   2.c. v^* is dual optimal for every non-negative final demand.

The main result is that if problem (2.2) is feasible for some $f > 0$, then a <u>pure</u> technology alternative exists that can produce <u>any</u> $f \geqslant 0$ at minimal costs. Although the model formulation allowed more than one technique for each product, one specific choice of techniques can realize any final demand $f \geqslant 0$ efficiently. Theorem (2.2) is a variant of the non-substitution theorem of Samuelson, who proved a similar result for input-output models with just one primary input and no joint production. Indeed, in our model each technique, activity yields one product type, and per product type all relevant primary input coefficients are replaced by one per-unit direct cost coefficient. Hence the model 'recognizes' one single primary input. (See Samuelson (1951)).

Furthermore, the price vector v^* as defined in Theorem 2.1 has a useful economic interpretation. The elements of v^* express the costs of producing the final demand on a per-unit basis, while taking into account the mutual deliveries of products within the firm under the given technology alternative. Therefore the price vector v^* can be called the vector of per-unit redistributed variable costs for the optimal technology alternative. Apparently, the per-unit redistributed variable costs of the optimal technology alternative do not depend on the actual amounts of products to be delivered. Note that they need not be computed separately, but follow immediately from the dual optimum to (2.2).

The above discussion on the existence of a cost minimizing technology alternative immediately leads to one particular technology alternative which is pure, too. However, the model formulation does not exclude combinations of two (or even more) techniques for one single product beforehand (simultaneous use of more than one technique per product). We may wonder if the solution of our LP problem (2.2) indeed leads to a pure cost-minimizing technology alternative.

Suppose the final demand is positive for at least one of the products. Introducing the extra assumption that every product is involved in the production of any other product, it can easily be demonstrated that each basic feasible solution to problem (2.2) applies exactly one technique per product. In the case of a unique optimum, the optimal solution coincides with one of the basic feasible solutions and thus corresponds to a pure technology alternative. In the case of alternative optima, the simplex method applied to (2.2) automatically comes up with a pure cost-minimizing technology alternative. In Appendix A the related mathematical analysis is given.

Until now, we have assumed that the firm has to meet a certain constant final demand, regardless of the revenues of selling these products. The last part of this section treats the more general situation in which the firm also decides which types of products it will sell and how much of each type, apart from choosing between techniques. Therefore the market prices have to be taken in account and we take maximization of revenues minus production costs as the objective.

Let $p = (p(1),...,p(\Phi))$ be the market-price vector, let $z = (z(1),...,z(\Phi))'$ be the vector of actual outside supply and let $f = (f(1),...,f(\Phi))'$ be (redefined as) the vector of maximum outside supply. Now our model becomes

$$\begin{aligned}
\text{Maximize} \quad & -c_{prod}\, x_{prod} + pz \\
\text{s.t.} \quad & (I_\Phi - D_{\Phi\Phi})\, x_{prod} - z = 0 \\
& z \leq f \\
& x_{prod},\, z \geq 0
\end{aligned} \qquad (2.3)$$

Problem (2.3) can be written as

$$\text{Maximize } pz - \text{Minimize } c_{prod} \, x_{prod}$$
$$\text{s.t.} \quad (I_\Phi - D_{\Phi\Phi}) \, x_{prod} = z$$
$$x_{prod} \geqslant 0$$
$$\text{s.t.} \quad z \leqslant f$$
$$z \geqslant 0 \tag{2.4}$$

For any feasible z the inner minimization problem is of the form (2.2). We assume that the inner problem is feasible for any $z \geqslant 0$. From Theorem 2.1 it follows that the inner minimization yields a solution value of the form $c^*(I-D^*)^{-1}z$. Here $\nu^* := c^*(I-D^*)^{-1}$ are the per-unit redistributed variable costs of a cost minimizing technology alternative. We know that $\overset{\cdot}{\nu}^*$ is independent of the units of products actually sold. But it is possible, that the per-unit redistributed variable costs of some market product are higher than its sales price. Because of the objective of the firm, profit maximization, this market product should not be supplied to the outside market. On the other hand, market products with a sales price exceeding the per-unit redistributed variable costs, should be sold as much as possible. From this reasoning, it is clear that either a market product X_ϕ is not sold at all, or its demand is fully satisfied. Formally, this result follows from the fact that (2.4) can be written as

$$\text{Maximize } (p - \nu^*)z \quad \text{s.t. } 0 \leqslant z \leqslant f \tag{2.5}$$

2.4. <u>Make-or-buy decisions for technical services</u>

The management of an organization is often confronted with the problem whether to make or to buy certain commodities. E.g. the computerization of the organization's administrative system could be performed by external experts or, alternatively, be the task of a special service department within the organization. The choice between these possibilities could be based mainly on qualitative criteria (absence of know-how or skilled labour within the firm versus special requirements related to other internal production processes in the firm). On the other hand, financial aspects are also important. Quantitative approaches to the make-or-buy problem are regularly reported on in the literature (Baker and Taylor (1979), Capettini and Salamon (1977), Kaplan (1973, 1982, ch. 11), Manes et al. (1982)). Especially in cases where reciprocal services exist (i.e. mutual deliveries between service departments), the question of whether to generate a service internally or to acquire the service externally, is not trivial.

Chronologically ordered, the research on the so-called reciprocal service-cost problem can be seen as a development from input-output to mixed-integer programming models. Manes et al. (1982) have reviewed this research and then included avoidable fixed costs in the model formulation. In the present section, we will adopt their mixed integer programming (MIP) approach and combine it with the (continuous) LP model for multiple techniques. As an intermediate step, make-or-buy decisions are treated in the case of a constant net demand for TS (cf. Manes et al. (1982)). Subsequently, the case where the net demand for these services depends on the number of produced market products is presented.

As noted before, we account for M technical services: $TS_1, \ldots, TS_m, \ldots, TS_M$. The net demand $b_0(m)$ for TS_m is defined as the amount of TS_m as required by the sector products. We require $b_0(m) > 0$. For some TS_m there are two possibilities:

1. TS_m is produced internally. The per-unit direct variable costs are $c_0(m)$ and the amount of internally produced TS_m is denoted by $x_0(m)$. If $x_0(m) > 0$, then the firm incurs a fixed cost equal to $C(m) > 0$ and the direct costs of internal production are $c_0(m)x_0(m) + C(m)$. Furthermore, internal production of TS_m requires an amount $D_{im}x_0(m)$ of TS_i, $i = 1,\ldots,M$, where the rate $D_{im} > 0$ is again referred to as an intermediate input coefficient.

2. TS_m is bought externally. The amount of externally bought TS_m is $y(m)$. The firm only incurs a variable cost equal to $d(m)y(m)$, where $d(m)$ is the external price of TS_m. If some TS is bought externally, it does not require input from other TS.

In the case of a known, constant net demand for TS, the problem of finding the optimal TS alternative can be represented by the following cost-minimizing MIP model:

Minimize $\qquad c_0 x_0 + dy + C\delta$

s.t. $\qquad (I - D_0)x_0 + y \qquad = b_0$

$\qquad\qquad\qquad x_0 \qquad - W\delta \leqslant 0$

x_0, $y \geqslant 0$; δ 0-1 vector $\hfill (2.6)$

Here c_0, x_0, d, y, C are the vectors corresponding to the $c_0(m)$, $x_0(m)$, $d(m)$, $y(m)$, $C(m)$, m=1,...,M. We require c_0, d, C, $b_0 > 0$. Matrix D_0 contains the coefficients D_{im}. We require that D_0 is such that $(I-D_0)^{-1}$ exists and $(I-D_0)^{-1} \geqslant 0$. Hence production of all TS-types internally is feasible. Finally, W is a large positive number and represents the maximum capacity of internal TS production. If some $x_0(m)$ is positive, the associated fixed cost $C(m) > 0$ is accounted for in the objective function, through $\delta(m) = 1$. Contrary to the continuous LP model of the previous section, the present MIP model does not automatically come up with the per-unit redistributed variable cost of the optimal TS alternative as, in principle, shadow prices are not computed. Secondly, the cost-minimizing TS alternative can become sub-optimal if the net demand for TS changes.

In our corporate model the net demand cannot be taken constant. Instead, we will assume that it is a linear, homogeneous function of the production intensities in the sector 'market products'. So

$$b_0(m) = \sum_{\phi=1}^{\Phi} \sum_{\psi=1}^{\Psi_\phi} D_{m\phi}(\psi)\, x_\phi(\psi), \hfill (2.7)$$

where the $D_{m\phi}(\psi) \geqslant 0$ are the per-unit requirements for TS_m of product ϕ under technique ψ. From this coupling equation, the interdependency between the sectors 'market products' and 'technical services' becomes apparent. Suppose that changes in the direct cost coefficients of some product cause a switch of techniques. This, in turn, changes the net demand for TS, thereby eventually causing a different choice of TS alternative.

General rules for these changes in technique and make-or-buy choice and their mutual dependence cannot be given. Therefore we integrate all alternatives in one overall formulation. Let matrix $D_{M\Phi}$ (cf. section

2.2) be (re)defined as the matrix of coupling coefficients $D_{m\phi}(\psi)$. Now combining the LP formulation for multiple techniques, i.e. (2.3), with the MIP formulation for make-or-buy decisions, i.e. (2.6), yields the following overall model:

$$
\begin{array}{lll}
\text{Maximize} & -c_{prod}\, x_{prod} + pz - & c_0 x_0 - dy - C\delta \\[4pt]
\text{s.t.} & (I_\phi - D_{\phi\phi})\, x_{prod} - z & = 0 \\[4pt]
& z & \leqslant f \\[4pt]
& -D_{M\phi}\, x_{prod} \quad + (I - D_0)x_0 + y & = 0 \\[4pt]
& x_0 \quad - W\delta \leqslant 0 \\[8pt]
& x_{prod},\; z,\; x_0,\; y \geqslant 0 \\[4pt]
& \delta \;\; 0\text{--}1 \text{ vector}
\end{array}
\tag{2.8}
$$

Similar to the case without TS, an optimal solution to problem (2.8) exists with the following properties:

1. It is sufficient to apply exactly one technique for each market product actually produced.

2. Market products are either sold maximally or not sold at all.

Moreover, we have:

3. Each TS is either produced internally or bought externally.

The formal proof of these conjectures is given in Appendix A.

Economically, this result should not be surprising. The model formulation includes all possible TS alternatives. Now consider one particular TS alternative and compute its vector of per-unit redistributed variable cost. Using the TS consumption matrix $D_{M\phi}$, we can add the TS costs to the direct costs of the market products. Altogether, for each TS alternative, the variable part of the TS costs can be viewed as direct costs. But then we have precisely the circumstances of section 2.3, where we concluded that only one technique per product had to be applied. Moreover, we can compute the per-unit redistributed variable costs (in which the variable TS costs are included!) and compare them with the sales prices. Product types with sales prices exceeding the per-unit redistributed variable costs, should be sold maximally. The other product types should not be sold at all. This reasoning holds for any TS alternative, so in particular it will hold for the firm-wide optimal TS alternative.

The optimization of MIP problem (2.8) can be described as follows. For each TS alternative, the 'profitable' market products are selected. Supplying them at the maximum level to the market yields a certain contribution to the profit. This contribution must be compared with the fixed costs of the current TS alternative. Finally, the TS alternative is chosen under which the contribution to the profit minus fixed costs is maximal. However, if this difference is negative for all TS alternatives, there will be no production at all.

2.5. Summary

In this chapter we made a start with the design of a general model of the firm. We concentrated on the production transformation processes and took the input-output model of the firm as a starting point for our presentation.

Because usually input factors can be combined in more than one way, we had to generalize the input-output framework. The problem of finding the lowest-cost technology alternative was represented by a cost-minimizing LP model. In order to take the sales prices for market products into consideration, we changed the formulation into a profit maximizing LP model.

As a second generalization of input-output modelling, we considered make-or-buy decisions for technical services. Firstly the case with a given, constant demand for TS was treated. Finally, the associated MIP model and the profit maximizing LP model concerning technology alternatives and sales activities were integrated into one formulation, as the demand level for TS usually depends on the activities in the sector market products.

CHAPTER THREE

THE MODEL OF THE FIRM:
COST ALLOCATIONS AND ORGANIZATIONAL STRUCTURE

3.1. Introduction

Up to here, we have mainly been concerned with more or less technological features as represented in our model of the firm. In this chapter,
we will discuss an important financial issue, viz. cost allocation, in
the context of the corporate model as developed in the previous chapter.
As noted there, we are considering a firm in which part of the activities can be labelled as 'general services' (abbreviated GS). The GS sector produces common goods, i.e. goods from which the firm as a whole
benefits. This gives rise to common costs. They may be variable in the
long run, but, in the short run, they are assumed to be entirely fixed.
Because output of GS is not supplied to the outside market, the common
costs must somehow be allocated.

Now we have arrived at the key problem in cost allocation, namely the
occurrence of a setting in which a need for allocation arises, although
the particular costs are non-separable, indivisible.

In the accounting literature, a large number of articles is devoted to
cost allocation problems in firms. Comprehensive surveys and discussions
concerning the subject can be found in Biddle and Steinberg (1985) and
Thomas (1977). It should be noted that these authors and especially
Demski and Kreps (1982) largely recommend the 'decision focus': the
analysis of cost allocation from an organizational and decision-making
point of view.

The contributions in the literature originate from several disciplines
and a wide variety in assumptions, definitions and methodologies can be
noticed. Consequently, some kind of uniform, systematic development of
concepts and definitions hardly exists. For this reason, we will provide
first a more precise description of what is meant by cost allocation
(section 3.2). Then three particular allocation methods are discussed,
as an illustration of the problem statement (section 3.3). In the second

half of the chapter, the link between cost allocation, managerial behaviour and organizational structure will be explored (section 3.4).
Finally, the relevant organizational features are added to the corporate
model (section 3.5).

3.2. Cost allocation problems

A very general indication of what is meant by a cost allocation is given
in the following

Definition 3.1:

A _cost allocation_ is the partitioning of a cost among a set of cost objects. In case all of the cost is allocated, no more and no less, we
speak of a _full cost allocation_ (or, equivalently, 'full costing').

In every cost allocation, three elements play a central role:
1. the total amount of costs to be allocated;
2. the cost objects among which the costs are to be allocated;
3. the allocation method or allocation basis that partitions the total
   cost.

The type of the costs may be such that they are not entirely separable,
divisible over the cost objects. Then a cost allocation _problem_ arises
due to the joint (common) nature of (part of) the costs. The literature
on this subject can be divided roughly into two classes, viz. joint cost
allocation and common cost allocation. In order to clarify this distinction, the terms joint cost and common cost will be defined.

Definition 3.2:

A _joint cost_ is a non-separable, indivisible cost due to a non-separable
production function which is defined on two or more products. Here the
products are the cost objects.

So joint costs are related to joint production (see Dopuch et al. (1982,
chapter 9)). After the split-off point, separately identifiable products
exist, which should jointly bear the costs incurred up to the split-off
point (example: petroleum refinery).

Definition 3.3:

A common cost is a non-separable, indivisible cost of two or more divisions (or departments). Here the divisions (or departments) are the cost objects.

The divisions could have produced a certain intermediate product or service independently, but apparently they had decided to act together. Hence they jointly incur the cost of their joint action.

The reader may convince himself that these separate definitions do not always guarantee an unambiguous answer to the question whether some non-separable cost is either joint or common. However, what is really important, is the apparent non-separability of costs, caused by the absence of properties which enable some natural allocation among cost objects. Lacking this natural allocation basis, one has to design ('invent') an allocation rule. It is evident that every allocation rule is subject to a certain degree of arbitrariness.

Definition 3.4:

A cost allocation problem asks for the design of an allocation rule (allocation method, allocation basis) to be used for the allocation of certain indivisible (joint, common) costs.

3.3. Three illustrative examples

The nature of the cost allocation literature varies from intuitive, pragmatic methods to pure theoretical (game-theoretical and axiomatic) approaches. See Young (1985) for a compendium. In the present section, three particular proposals will be reviewed, both the allocation method itself and the setting in which it is needed.

3.3.1. The Louderback-Moriarity approach

Consider a firm consisting of N divisions each of which has to supply a certain quantity of a product. There exist three ways to fulfil this task.

In the first production possibility, the divisions jointly buy an amount of raw material, then extract N intermediate products (costs: C_0) to be further processed by the divisions independently. A division finishing its own product incurs a cost equal to C_n. The total cost of this production possibility is thus: $C_0 + C_1 + \ldots + C_N$.

Secondly, each division has the opportunity to buy the required quantity of its final product independently. This costs: Y_n, $n = 1,\ldots,N$.

One could also imagine that the finishing cost C_n of some division n is so low that this division is tempted to buy the same amount of raw material entirely for itself, and then extract and finish its product. The cost then is $C_0 + C_n$, as it is assumed impossible to buy smaller (and hence cheaper) amounts of the raw material.

It will be assumed that the first option, i.e. jointly buying the raw material and then further processing by individual divisions, is the cheapest alternative, so $C_0 + C_1 + \ldots + C_N < Y_1 + \ldots + Y_N$. Furthermore, every division has a potential interest for this option, as for every division the finishing cost is lower than the cost of buying the product independently. Formally: $C_n < Y_n$ for $n = 1,\ldots,N$.

For the firm as a whole, the alternative according to which all divisions jointly use the raw material is the most attractive one. Below we describe an allocation rule which stimulates divisions to join in the common purchase and use of the raw material. Note that in this setting the common costs arise because of cost savings.

Balachandran and Ramakrishnan (1981) discuss the allocation problem outlined above, partly inspired by the contributions of Moriarity (1975, 1976) and Louderback (1976). The proposed allocation rule, to be referred to as the Louderback-Moriarity method, can be stated as follows.

Let Z_n be the cost of the n-th division's next-best alternative. Since a division might be tempted to buy the raw material independently, it holds that $Z_n = \min \{Y_n, C_0 + C_n\}$. Let TOTAL denote the total cost to be allocated, i.e. TOTAL $= C_0 + C_1 + \ldots + C_N$, and let G_n be the cost allocated to division n ($n = 1,\ldots,N$). Now the allocation rule is:

$$G_n = C_n + (\text{TOTAL} - \sum_{n=1}^{N} C_n) \frac{Z_n - C_n}{\sum_{n=1}^{N} (Z_n - C_n)} \tag{3.1}$$

C_n is a sort of 'basic charge', while $Z_n - C_n$ can be seen as the 'propensity to contribute'.

The allocation rule (3.1) has some attractive properties. Every division is encouraged to take part in the joint use of the raw material (because $G_n \leqslant Z_n$) and has a positive share in the savings of the entire firm. No division is subsidized: its part of the total costs is at least as much as its own costs. Every division is tempted to look for cheaper next-best alternatives, as that would reduce its relative propensity to contribute. The same holds with respect to the division's finishing cost C_n: finding cheaper finishing technologies results in a lower basic charge.

What we find interesting in the propensity to contribute concept, is the observation of a margin between a division's basic charge and the cost of its next-best alternative. The allocation of cost savings in proportion to the division's margin $Z_n - C_n$ can be viewed as a fairness requirement. Nevertheless, this interpretation of fairness is more or less arbitrary. The division's margin could have been utilized in a different way.

3.3.2. The reciprocal allocation method

The Louderback–Moriarity method is concerned with allocating the savings of one particular joint facility (namely the joint purchase of a common raw material). No distinction is made between fixed and variable costs. Now we treat a more complex situation with a number of joint facilities, say technical services (TS), which incur fixed and variable costs. Each TS is supplied to the divisions but the TS departments also deliver services to each other. E.g. the data processing department provides output for many TS departments. It is the latter feature that makes cost allocation to users (divisions and TS departments!) essentially more difficult. For a TS department supplying not only to divisions but also to itself and other TS departments, must reasonably allocate part of its total cost to these TS departments. But this part of the cost allocation is of a reciprocal nature, so that the 'total cost' is not known in advance and actually depends on the allocation itself.

In order to cope with this effect, a method is proposed that computes the allocations on a basis of usage, through a set of simultaneous equations. As a result, both total costs, the so-called redistributed costs, and their allocation over all consumers (including TS departments) are obtained simultaneously. Below we will summarize this method by giving the main formulas and their meanings. See also Kaplan (1982, ch. 11). It should be noted that the reciprocal allocation method implicitly assumes financial reporting on an input-output basis. In particular, it is presumed that the deliveries between the TS departments can be characterized by a matrix D_0 with intermediate input coefficients (cf. section 2.4).

Now let x_0 denote the total production of TS. Define the diagonal matrix $\text{diag}[x_0]$ by $\text{diag}[x_0]_{mm} := x_0(m)$, $m = 1,\ldots,M$. Here M is again the number of different TS and we assume that all $x_0(m) > 0$. The row vectors c_0' and C' contain the per-unit direct variable cost coefficients and the fixed costs, respectively. The price $g(m)$ charged to the users of service m is the m-th element of the row vector g' defined by

$$g' := (c_0' + C'\ \text{diag}^{-1}[x_0])\ (I-D_0)^{-1} \tag{3.2}$$

Vector g' is called the vector of per-unit redistributed costs. The terms $c_0' + C'\text{diag}^{-1}[x_0]$ contain the direct variable and fixed costs respectively, both on a per-unit basis. Multiplication with $(I - D_0)^{-1}$ redistributes the direct costs on the basis of input coefficients as contained in matrix D_0, and thus on a usage basis.

We see that the indivisibility of the fixed costs is resolved by an appropriate modification of the vector of direct cost coefficients. If we multiply both sides of (3.2) with $\text{diag}[x_0]$, we obtain the above mentioned redistributed costs G'. Hence, the row vector of redistributed costs G' is given by

$$G' := (c_0' + C'\ \text{diag}^{-1}[x_0])\ (I-D_0)^{-1}\text{diag}[x_0] \tag{3.3}$$

To conclude, a few considerations are in order concerning the motives for allocating TS costs. TS departments are typically cost centres, as they do not produce for the market. We fully agree with Kaplan (1982, ch. 11), who argues that charging the (profit-conscious!) divisions for their use of TS may well stimulate prudent usage of TS. In turn, the divisional managers will provide signals on the quality of the services obtained. Because the reciprocal allocation method correctly treats the mutual deliveries between TS departments, it facilitates comparison with externally supplied services. Altogether, allocating TS costs provides incentives to the TS departments to operate efficiently and to satisfy the demands of their users.

3.3.3. Fixed cost allocation via mathematical programming

Kaplan and Thompson (1971) have described how a fixed overhead cost can be allocated among activities in the context of a linear programming (LP) model of the firm, without distorting the relative profitability of products. Below, we will discuss their contribution, as we also apply a mathematical programming approach to corporate modelling.

Suppose that the LP problem

$$
\begin{aligned}
\text{Maximize } & px \\
\text{s.t.} \quad & Ax \leq a \\
& Bx \leq b \\
& x \geq 0
\end{aligned}
\tag{3.4}
$$

formally represents the planning problem the firm is faced with. Furthermore, suppose the management of the firm has solved (3.4). The objective of the firm is profit maximization and the first set of constraints, i.e. $Ax \leq a$, are associated with certain resources which are available in limited amounts. Having solved (3.4) the management knows an optimal plan $\bar{x}$, maximum profit OPT if this plan is carried out, and a valuation $\bar{\pi}a$ of the scarce resources just mentioned. (Here $\bar{\pi}$ is an optimal dual variable associated to constraints $Ax \leq a$. We assume that OPT is ≥ 0 and finite.)

Now, as a second step, the management may want to allocate fixed costs, like overhead costs, depreciation of machinery or another kind of common costs. Let the total costs to be allocated, say H (≥ 0), be smaller than the valuation of the scarce resources, i.e. $H \leq \bar{\pi}a$. Then these costs can be allocated as follows.

Compute the fraction $h := H/(\bar{\pi}a)$ (so $0 < h < 1$). Each feasible plan x captures a particular set of activities that can be performed by the firm and requires an amount Ax of the scarce resources. Now charge this claim on scarce resources with per-unit prices, namely the elements of price vector $h\bar{\pi}$. This implies that plan x will be allocated a cost equal to $h\bar{\pi}Ax$. Subsequently, find a feasible plan that maximizes the profit given these per-unit charges on scarce resources. Formally, the following LP problem has to be solved:

$$\text{Maximize } (p - \bar{h\pi}A)x$$
$$\text{s.t.} \qquad Ax \leqslant a$$
$$Bx \leqslant b$$
$$x \geqslant 0 \tag{3.5}$$

In Appendix B it is proved that the originally optimal plan, i.e. $\bar{x}$, is again optimal in the new situation. Moreover, it realizes a profit that is equal to $OPT - h\bar{\pi}a = OPT - H$. So the original (gross) profit, i.e. OPT, is maintained while the common costs H are fully allocated.

3.4. Cost allocation and multilevel decisions

In this section we will clarify that cost allocation, as defined and illustrated in the two preceding sections, has an strong relationship with the organizational structure of and the decision-making in the firm. In this light two interesting publications are then reviewed.

3.4.1. Motives for the analysis of allocation problems

A firm faces allocation problems whenever joint or common costs are incurred. Recalling the organizational setting in the Louderback-Moriarity approach, we observe that common costs often arise because of cost savings due to joint action (instead of independent behaviour of the cost objects). A second source of joint costs is the occurrence of internal 'general services' like central management, research and development, public relations. These departments produce common goods from which all other subunits in the firm benefit, thereby giving rise to common costs to be borne by the firm as a whole.

From an overall point of view, i.e. if some overall optimization model for the entire firm is applied, it is often concluded that allocation should not be taken into account. Discussions and more references on this theoretical result can be found in Biddle and Steinberg (1985, p. 34) and Thomas (1977, p. 5). Briefly speaking, a substantial part of the literature suggests 'allocation free' corporate models. But, at the same time, we observe that in any organization of a reasonable size a certain degree of decentralization has taken place. The information necessary to make decisions is dispersed among the subunits within the firm (localized information) and, in order to reduce the complexity in managing the whole enterprise, decision-making authority is delegated to lower levels in the organization. This implies that the use of overall optimization problems as models for a decentralized firm is highly unrealistic. As a consequence, different types of models are required explicitly recognizing the decentralization features. It is not a priori clear whether these models again turn out to be allocation free. In summary, the theoretical justification for not considering cost allocation may well be non-valid in more decentralized settings.

The potential theoretical improvements by the explicit recognition of allocation issues in modelling complex, decentralized organizations can be of practical significance, as common cost allocations actually occur in multi-division firms. The third and probably most important motive, which is again inspired by decentralization, is that, whenever a process of delegation of decision authority occurs, the division managers become local decision-makers with their own responsibilities, goals and preferences. Now a motivation and a coordination problem arises, as Dopuch et al. (1982, p. 330) notes. How can local decision-makers be lead towards firm-wide optimal decisions? Thomas (1977, pp. 7-8) provides reasonable arguments why the decision of a division manager may be affected by allocated costs. As an example, we return to the Louderback-Moriarity approach. The proposed allocation method clearly stimulates divisions to joint action and implicitly assumes that the cost allocation has an effect on the behaviour of a division manager (e.g. looking for cheaper next-best alternatives).

3.4.2. <u>Cost allocation in a decentralized organizational structure</u>

Altogether, in a multi-division setting, common-cost allocation is not only likely to occur, but will have an effect on the decision-making within the firm. This provides a strong incentive to look for allocation rules which are consistent with the organizational structure. Therefore, we review two contributions in the literature that incorporate organizational considerations.

Zimmerman (1979, p. 505) observes that "cost allocations, managerial behavior, and the structure of the organization, including the incentives facing the managers, are extricably linked". In his article, Zimmerman states that in certain situations cost allocations yield positive net benefits to the firm. This notion is further explored by indicating the relationship with the agency problem. A second topic in his presentation refers to situations where allocated costs are coupled to the use a division makes of production factors (e.g. labour). This kind of allocations are sometimes observed in practice, and may induce divisions to switch to labour-extensive production technologies, which in turn can be sub-optimal from a firm-wide point of view.

Contrary to Zimmerman's set up, which is of a more or less descriptive, introductory kind, Cohen and Loeb (1982) provide a formal approach to common cost allocation in a divisionalized firm. They start with the characterization of a pure common good: once produced, it is free for all divisions to consume. (Example: corporate image advertising.) The opposite of a pure common good is a pure private good: once consumed by some division, it is not available anymore to other divisions. (Example: collective typing service department in a university.) While Hughes and Scheiner (1980, p. 90) proved that no full cost allocation scheme exists for pure private goods which enhances "efficient decentralization", Cohen et al. shows "that it is possible to reach an efficient allocation by decentralization and fully allocating costs" in the case of purely common goods. Here 'efficient' refers to the performance of the firm as a whole.

The organizational model of Cohen and Loeb consists of a number of divisions plus corporate headquarters. The divisions all require a certain purely common input which is to be delivered by headquarters. The provision of the common input leads to common costs incurred by headquarters, and to be allocated to the divisions which are considered as profit centers. Having incomplete information with respect to the divisional profit functions, it is difficult for headquarters to determine the right level of the common input. The allocations of the common costs should generate information about divisional demand and thus be helpful in choosing the optimal level of the common input.

It is not the right place here to present the complete model as developed by Cohen and Loeb. The main result is that the divisions are charged according to the marginal benefits they receive from the common input. This brings about the 'free-rider problem': divisions have the tendency to understate their demands and still enjoy the benefits of the common good.

3.5. The overall model

The aim of this book is to investigate two-level planning in decentralized enterprises. To this end, we started to design a general model of the firm. In chapter 2, the input-output model of the firm was generalized with multiple technologies and make-or-buy decisions, thus leading to a mixed-integer programming (MIP) formulation. In the present chapter, the third issue to be included was introduced, namely cost allocation. Cost allocation problems appeared to be closely related to the organizational structure of companies. Therefore, to complete our model of the firm, we will now add the necessary organizational features.

We consider a firm in which two sorts of subunits, viz. divisions and departments, can be distinguished.

The divisions produce the commodities that can be sold on the external market (i.e. the actual output of the firm) and are profit centres. The divisionalization is based on the joining of related market products: per division we have market products whose production processes are highly interdependent. Because there is no direct connection between production processes in different divisions, they operate relatively independently of each other and can freely choose among a number of technology alternatives in producing their output.

To do their task, the divisions require technical services (TS) either bought externally, from outside suppliers, or produced internally, in the TS departments.

A second interdependency between divisions is the common use of certain resources, each with fixed capacity, to be referred to as common resources (CR). The way in which CR is partitioned among the divisions influences their production possibilities and hence their contributions to the profit.

The latter property provides the essential distinction with those internal facilities and activities that we have defined as general services (GS). The GS departments perform actions that do not affect the production of products and services in the short run. The only problem is the allocation of their (constant) costs, the common costs, without distorting firm-wide desired technology and make-or-buy decisions.

The divisions and departments are coordinated by the so-called <u>central unit</u>. As part of the top management of the firm, the central unit is responsible for the total net profit, which is, by definition, equal to the sum of the divisional profits minus internal-TS costs and common costs. The central unit must find the optimal partitioning of CR among the divisions. Furthermore, it is in charge of the allocation of costs, namely the internal-TS costs and the common costs.

The decision-making process in the firm is organized according to the following two-level structure:
- At the lower level, we have the divisions. Each of them possesses the specific knowledge with respect to available techniques, market restrictions etc., not known to other subunits.
- At the higher level, we have the central unit. It directly controls the departments and the consumption of CR, but does not have complete information on the divisions.

Thus, the divisional two-level structure reflects the specialization and the localized information in the firm.

Now we turn to the formal presentation of the model. Similar to section 2.4, a MIP formulation is proposed, but from now on the structure of the constraints clearly expresses the divisionalization. In table 3.1 (see page 36) the MIP model is given. Below, the meaning of the symbols in this problem formulation will be clarified. A notational convention to be used throughout the book is that scalar-valued elements of vectors are usually indicated by an appropriate index between brackets.

There are N divisions, to be indicated by index n. The total production vector x_{prod}, as introduced in section 2.3, is replaced by $x_1,\ldots,x_N$ and each x_n is now the total production vector of division n. Similarly, $c_1,\ldots,c_N$ replace c_{prod}. The sales level, the maximum outside supply and the sales prices are indexed per division: z_n, f_n and p_n. Division n produces and sells Φ_n product types: $X_{n,\phi}$, $\phi=1,\ldots,\Phi_n$. For each product type, $\Psi_{n,\phi}$ production techniques exist. Let $x_{n,\phi}(\psi)$ denote the units of produced $X_{n,\phi}$ by applying technique ψ, $\psi=1,\ldots,\Psi_{n,\phi}$. The production vector $x_{n,\phi}$ for product type $X_{n,\phi}$ is defined by $x_{n,\phi} := (x_{n,\phi}(1),\ldots,x_{n,\phi}(\psi),\ldots,x_{n,\phi}(\psi_{n,\phi}))'$. Thus, instead of Φ, X_ϕ, ψ_ϕ, $x_\phi(\psi)$, x_ϕ (as used in chapter two), we have:

Φ_n := number of product types in division n,

$X_{n,\phi}$:= product type ϕ in division n,

$\Psi_{n,\phi}$:= number of techniques for product type $X_{n,\phi}$,

$x_{n,\phi}(\psi)$:= units of produced $X_{n,\phi}$ by using technique ψ,

$x_{n,\phi}$:= production vector for product type $X_{n,\phi}$.

These definitions can be illustrated as follows

total production $x_1,\ldots,x_n,\ldots,x_N$

production vector $x_n = (x'_{n,1},\ldots,x'_{n,\phi},\ldots,x'_{n,\Phi_n})'$
of division n

production vector $x'_{n,\phi} = (x_{n,\phi}(1),\ldots,x_{n,\phi}(\psi),\ldots,x_{n,\phi}(\Psi_{n,\phi}))$
of product type $X_{n,\phi}$

Maximize s.t.	$-c_1x_1 - dy_1 + P_1z_1$ A_1x_1	$-c_2x_2 - dy_2 + P_2z_2$ $+ A_2x_2$	$\cdots$	$-c_Nx_N - dy_N + P_Nz_N$ $+ A_Nx_N$	$-c_0x_0 - dy_0 - C\delta$	$\leqslant a$
	$B_1x_1 - y_1$ $(I_1 - D_1)x_1 - z_1$ z_1				$- b_1$	$\leqslant 0$ $= 0$ $\leqslant f_1$
		$B_2x_2 - y_2$ $(I_2 - D_2)x_2 - z_2$ z_2			$- b_2$	$\leqslant 0$ $= 0$ $\leqslant f_2$
			$\cdot\cdot\cdot$			$\cdot$ $\cdot$ $\cdot$
				$B_Nx_N - y_N$ $(I_N - D_N)x_N - z_N$ z_N	$- b_N$	$\leqslant 0$ $= 0$ $\leqslant f_N$
					$b_1 + b_2 \cdots + b_N - b_0$ $b_0 - (I - D_0)x_0 - y_0$ $b_0 \quad - W\delta$ $x_0 \quad - W\delta$	$= 0$ $= 0$ $\leqslant 0$ $\leqslant 0$

all x_n, y_n, z_n, $b_n \geqslant 0$

δ : 0-1 vector

W : large positive constant

Table 3.1: Problem (3.6): the MIP formulation of the two-level
divisionalized firm.

The matrices $I_n - D_n$, $n = 1,\ldots,N$, replace $I_\phi - D_{\phi\phi}$. Here $D_n :=$ $(D_{n,1} \mid \ldots \mid D_{n,\Phi_n})$ and $D_{n,\phi}$ contains all $\psi_{n,\phi}$ columns of intermediate input coefficients for product type $X_{n,\phi}$. So D_n has Φ_n rows and $\sum_{\phi=1}^{\Phi_n} \psi_{n,\phi}$ columns, and I_n is a 'generalized' identity matrix of the same dimension:

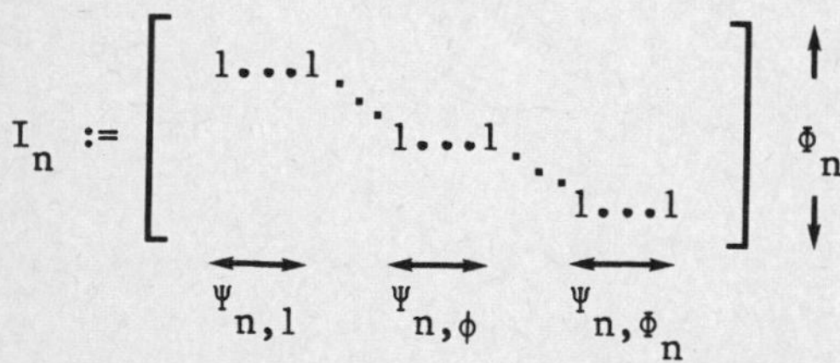

It is assumed that only production (and not sales) activities require CR and TS. The per-unit CR and TS inputs are given through the matrices A_n and B_n, respectively. The right-hand side vector 'a' reflects the fixed capacities for CR, whereas TS can be bought externally (y_n), at prices d, or internally produced (x_0) and supplied (b_n) to divisions.

The notation with respect to the TS sector is almost the same as in section 2.4. The differences are now given. Instead of y, we have $y_1,\ldots,y_N$ for externally bought TS in divisions, and y_0. Here y_0 is not yet defined: $y_0(m)$ is the amount of externally bought TS_m as used in the internal production of other TS, so <u>not</u> available for divisions.

Vector δ has two functions. Firstly, it still guarantees that, whenever $x_0(m) > 0$, the related fixed cost $C(m)$ is accounted for in the objective function. Secondly, by the constraints $b_0(m) - W\delta(m) \leqslant 0$ and $b_0(m) \geqslant 0$, it is guaranteed that $x_0(m) = 0$ implies $b_0(m) = 0$. So, if TS_m is not produced internally, then there is no internal flow of TS_m towards divisions; they have to buy TS_m from outside the firm independently.

Finally, it is required that the central unit cannot obtain external TS via the divisions; it has to buy external TS directly from outside the firm, without interference of divisions. Therefore $b_1,\ldots,b_N$ are non-negative.

With respect to the objective function, we note that the common costs are not included as they were assumed to be entirely constant.

Altogether, the development of our general model of the firm is completed now. The management of the firm is faced with a complex planning problem that consists of two parts namely:

1. The problem of determining firm-wide optimal production techniques and make-or-buy decisions without overconsumption of the common resources. This problem is formally represented by the MIP problem in table 3.1. Moreover, the constraints of the MIP formulation reflect the divisional organization structure.
2. The problem of allocating the common costs and the costs of producing TS internally.

Under complete information, the central unit can immediately solve the MIP problem and then (try to) allocate costs such that divisional managers have no intention to object against the firm-wide optimal decisions. In reality, however, the information needed to solve the planning problem is dispersed among the subunits of the firm. Because of the two-level, divisional organization al structure, decomposition-based planning procedures can be applied. The next two chapters are devoted to these solution methods which fit into the information dispersal in the firm.

3.6. <u>Summary</u>

In many firms activities of the kind 'general services' lead to common costs to be beared by the firm as a whole. Secondly, the costs of internally produced TS must be allocated to consumers of these services. Therefore we discussed the issue of cost allocation as a financial aspect of decentralized enterprises to be accounted for in our model. We stated the necessary definitions and provided three illustrative examples.

So, after investigating technological features in chapter two, we continued with an important financial issue which is closely related to the organizational structure of the firm. We concluded the chapter with the description and formalization of organizational features that are incorporated in our model of the firm.

CHAPTER FOUR

DECOMPOSITION BASED PLANNING:
PRICE AND RESOURCE DIRECTIVE COORDINATION

4.1. Introduction

In the two preceding chapters the model of a general, two-level divisionalized firm has been developed. The top management is faced with a
planning problem, the first technological part of which is mathematically represented by a MIP problem formulation. The constraints of this MIP
model have a special structure which corresponds to the divisionalization in the firm.

Two-level decentralized organizations are often represented formally
by mathematical programming problems with a similar block-angular structure. However, these formulations may lead to large problems. In the
late fifties, solution techniques have been developed by which the
original problem is decomposed into a number of subproblems of smaller
size. This approach was necessitated by the limited capacities of com-
puters in that period. Nowadays, the computational importance of these
decomposition methods has decreased. On the other hand, the algorithms
appear to have a straightforward economic interpretation; they resemble
planning procedures in multilevel organizations.

Thus, by studying decomposition methods from an economic point of
view, planning processes in two-level, decentralized organizations can
be analysed. Examples in the field of corporate planning are, e.g.
Dirickx and Jennergren (1979, ch. 6), Obel (1981). Similarly, for
national planning we mention Dirickx and Jennergren (1979, ch. 5),
Johansen (1978, ch. 5).

In the present and the next chapter, decomposable LP problems are investigated. We consider decomposition methods that are somehow consistent with the information dispersal in the organization at hand. It is
not our purpose to provide a broad overview of all kinds of models, nor
to describe and interpret the mathematical solution techniques extensively. Useful surveys, especially with respect to algorithmic details
and variants, can be found in the literature (Geoffrion (1970-b),

Himmelblau (1972), Luna (1984), Molina (1979), Ruefli (1974)). As part of the mathematical programming approach to organizational design, we merely intend to illustrate the value of decomposable models when investigating multilevel organizations. Therefore we restrict the presentation to one price-directive (section 4.3) and one resource-directive decomposition technique (section 4.4). First of all, a more precise problem statement for chapters four and five is given.

4.2. The planning problem

The problems to be analysed are of the form:

$$
\begin{aligned}
\text{Maximize } & p_1 x_1 + \ldots + p_N x_N \\
\text{s.t.} \quad & A_1 x_1 + \ldots + A_N x_N \leq a \\
& Q_1 x_1 \qquad\qquad\qquad \leq q_1 \\
& \qquad \ddots \qquad\qquad\quad \vdots \\
& \qquad\qquad\quad Q_N x_N \leq q_N \\
& x_1, \ldots, x_N \geq 0
\end{aligned}
\tag{4.1}
$$

Here a, q_n, p_n are constant vectors, A_n, Q_n are constant matrices and x_n is a variable vector, all of appropriate dimensions ($n=1,\ldots,N$). The variables are assumed to be continuous.

Even without the knowledge of chapters two and three, the problem formulation (4.1) can be recognized as an abstraction of the planning problem in a decentralized organization. A reasonable economic interpretation, which we will consequently apply in this and the following chapter, is now given.

Blocks $Q_n x_n \leq q_n$, $x_n \geq 0$ ($n=1,\ldots,N$) are associated with N divisions, at the lower level in the organization. Vector x_n represents the activities of a division (purchase of raw materials, production, deliveries to other divisions, sales to outside customers). The local constraints $Q_n x_n \leq q_n$ refer to, for example, capacity constraints, maximum/minimum supply to customers, and $p_n x_n$ is the divisional contribution to profit.

The common constraints $A_1 x_1 + \ldots + A_N x_N \leq a$ reflect interdependencies between divisions, such as mutual deliveries of semifinished products, and common use of machinery and manpower. In our presentation, the common constraints will usually be interpreted in terms of 'common use of scarce resources'. We will assume that, at the higher level in the organization, there is a central unit that distributes these common resources (CR) to the N divisions. Hence, problem (4.1) will be viewed as a <u>resource allocation</u> problem.

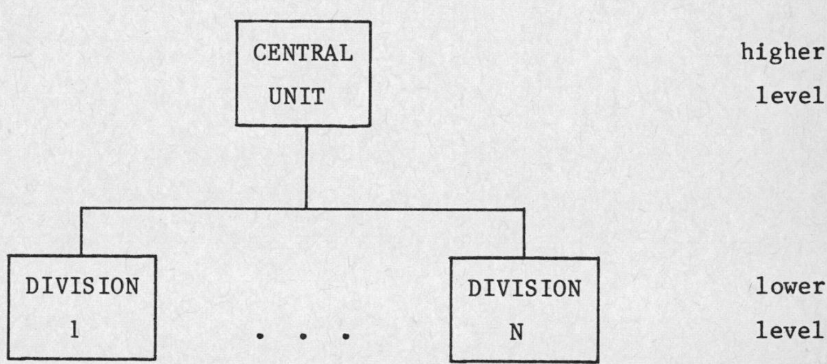

<u>Figure 4.1</u>: Organizational structure underlying the formal problem formulation (4.1)

In fact the central unit is faced with the following problem. Determine an allocation of the common resources such that optimal utilization of the allocated CR in each division yields divisional production plans which are also optimal from a firm-wide point of view. Formally: choose $\bar{a}_1,\ldots,\bar{a}_N$ with $\bar{a}_1 + \ldots + \bar{a}_N = a$, such that if for $n=1,\ldots,N$ $\hat{x}_n$ is optimal to

$$
\begin{aligned}
\text{Maximize } & p_n x_n \\
\text{s.t.} \quad & A_n x_n \leqslant \bar{a}_n \\
& Q_n x_n \leqslant q_n \\
& x_n \geqslant 0
\end{aligned}
\tag{4.2}
$$

the set of divisional solutions $\hat{x}_n$ forms a solution $\hat{x}_1,\ldots,\hat{x}_N$ that is optimal to the original problem (4.1).

The central unit cannot solve the overall planning problem (4.1) itself because it lacks essential pieces of information concerning the divisions. Reversely, the divisions do not have the specification of the common constraints. In order to be able to solve the planning problem, i.e. before decisions can actually be made, the central unit must gather the necessary information. This will be accomplished in the form of a planning procedure.

The term 'planning' requires some clarification. We consider planning as one of the stages in the entire process of decision-making. A <u>deci-sion-making process</u> is, in turn, defined as the whole process of solving a problem related to the organization and then making sure that actions are carried out according to this solution. Now, several stages may be distinguished: (1) initialization, (2) planning, (3) implementation, (4) control and/or evaluation. See e.g. Obel (1981, pp. 65-71). In this book, we are mainly concerned with the <u>planning phase</u>, i.e. the phase in a decision-making process that involves the search for the decision to be made and carried out.

Because of the incomplete information at the higher level in the organization, we propose decomposition-based planning procedures. This implies that the overall problem is broken down, decomposed into a number of subproblems of reduced size and complexity. Each subproblem is related to a subunit in the organization. Moreover:

1. The decomposition methods to be presented are two-level methods. Each subproblem related to a subunit at the lower level in the organization has its own coefficients, which do not occur in the other subproblems. This means that we can handle a firm in which divisions possess technological knowledge and local information, not known or relevant to other divisions and/or the central unit.

2. During the steps of the procedure, parameters are exchanged between subproblems related to different levels. This can be interpreted as information exchange between hierarchical levels for planning purposes.

3. In decomposition-based planning procedures coordination is accomplished by prices (e.g. Dantzig (1963, ch. 23)), direct allocations (e.g. Benders (1962), Ten Kate (1972)) or a combination of the two (Obel (1978), Shapiro and White (1982)). In real organizations transfer prices and budgets are often used as coordinating instruments.

In the present chapter these features are further elaborated. Mixed price-resource directive approaches will be discussed in chapter five.

4.3. <u>Price-directive planning according to the Dantzig-Wolfe decomposition method</u>

This section is devoted to a planning procedure based on the famous decomposition method of Dantzig-Wolfe (see Dantzig (1963, ch. 23)). In a sequence of planning sessions the central unit announces tentative prices for common resources to the divisions. From the divisional responses, i.e. tentative production plans with associated profit, the central unit extends its (ever incomplete) information on local circumstances. Below we present a more detailed description of the procedure. The underlying mathematics can be found in Appendix C.

At the beginning of a new planning session the central unit announces tentative prices $\bar{\pi}_0$ for CR. Each division is asked to report a (tentative) production plan $\hat{x}_n^i$ that would yield a maximal profit $\hat{P}_n$ given these prices for CR. Formally, each division solves

$$\text{Maximize } (p_n - \bar{\pi}_0 A_n)x_n$$
$$\text{s.t.} \qquad Q_n x_n \leq q_n$$
$$x_n \geq 0 \qquad\qquad\qquad (4.3)$$

and reports an extreme point $\hat{x}_n^i$ of the feasible region (which is assumed to be bounded) where the optimal solution value $\hat{P}_n$ is attained.

The central unit actually solves a sort of reformulated version of the original problem (4.1), viz.

$$\text{Maximize } \sum_{n=1}^{N} \sum_{i=1}^{\bar{S}_n} p_n^i \lambda_n^i$$
$$\text{s.t.} \qquad \sum_{n=1}^{N} \sum_{i=1}^{\bar{S}_n} A_n^i \lambda_n^i \leq a$$
$$\sum_{i=1}^{\bar{S}_n} \lambda_n^i = 1 \ , \ n = 1,\ldots,N$$
$$\text{all } \lambda_n^i \geq 0 \qquad\qquad\qquad (4.4)$$

Here $p_n^i := p_n x_n^i$ and $A_n^i := A_n x_n^i$ ($i=1,\ldots,\bar{S}_n$, $n=1,\ldots,N$), where, in turn, $\{x_n^i \mid i=1,\ldots,\bar{S}_n\}$ denotes only subset of the extreme points of the n-th division's feasible region ($n=1,\ldots,N$). So problem (4.4) does not take account all divisional extreme points. This represents the fact that the central unit has incomplete information on the divisions and thus cannot know all extreme points of each division.

However, through the succession of a number of planning sessions, the central unit gathers a subset of each division's set of extreme points. So at any point in the planning process, the central unit knows part of the divisional production possibilities in terms of a convex subset of each divisional feasible region. Therefore solutions based on this partial information and subject to the constraints for CR will always be firm-wide feasible. But even the best solution (i.e. the optimal solution to problem (4.4)) may well be sub-optimal, because not all divisional production possibilities are accounted for. In particular, the total profit as 'estimated' by the central unit is a lower bound of the actual (but still unknown) total profit. Moreover, the sequence of lower bounds as generated during the planning procedure is increasing, because the central unit has more and more information on feasible production possibilities. At each stage in the solution process, the central unit can derive an intermediate solution to the original problem (4.1) by formula

$$\bar{x}_n := \sum_{i=1}^{\bar{S}_n} \bar{\lambda}_n^i x_n^i, \quad n = 1,\ldots,N \tag{4.5}$$

Here $\bar{\lambda}_n^i$, $i=1,\ldots,\bar{S}_n$, $n=1,\ldots,N$, denote the solution to the current version of problem (4.4).

When computing the best solution given the incomplete information, the central unit obtains a shadow price for CR. The central unit uses this price, say $\bar{\pi}_0$, as a tentative price (a sort of transfer price) for CR. From the modified divisional profit function (see (4.3)), we see that the term $-\bar{\pi}_0 A_n$ acts as a penalty cost for consuming CR. The divisional responses (formally, $\hat{x}_n^i$) are locally optimal plan proposals given the current prices $\bar{\pi}_0$ for CR. So the response on price information, by the central unit, is quantity information, by the divisions. See figure 4.2.

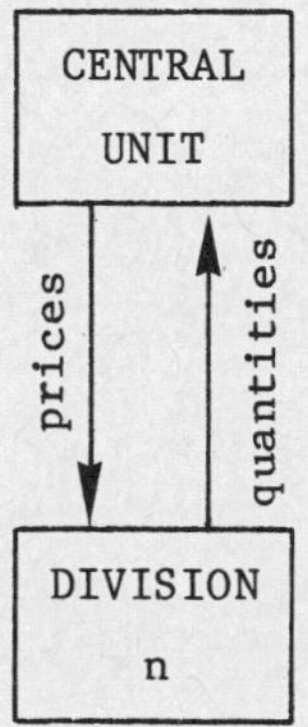

Figure 4.2: Information exchange in the price-directive planning procedure according to Dantzig-Wolfe.

The use of centrally computed shadow prices for CR as tentative transfer prices can be explained as follows.

Consider an optimal solution to the current version of problem (4.4), say the current central solution. Let $\bar{\omega}_n$, $n=1,\ldots,N$, denote the optimal dual variables associated with the equality constraints in problem (4.4). Basic columns of problem (4.4) correspond to extreme points already generated <u>and</u> used in the current central solution, say 'basic revealed extreme points'. Now the following relationship holds for basic revealed extreme points: $(p_n - \bar{\pi}_0 A_n)x_n^i = \bar{\omega}_n$. As noted before, $\bar{\pi}_0 A_n$ equals the cost for using CR. Therefore $\bar{\omega}_n$ can be seen as the net profit contribution of basic revealed extreme points.

The central unit checks whether a division can offer plan proposals the net profit contribution of which is larger than the contribution of the optimally combined plan proposals as previously offered by that division. In particular, the central unit asks for the plan proposal which has a net contribution to profit that maximally exceeds the current net contribution. (Formally, for which n is $\hat{P}_n > \bar{\omega}_n$?) If no division provides improving proposals (i.e. all $\hat{P}_n < \bar{\omega}_n$) , the procedure can be terminated. Otherwise the central unit updates its information by adding the latest plan proposals, and starts a new planning session.

4.4. Resource-directive planning according to Benders' decomposition method

The resource-directive planning procedure to be presented here is based on the partitioning procedure for solving mixed-variables programming problems as developed by Benders (1962). In a sequence of planning sessions the central unit announces tentative portions, allocations of CR to the divisions. Each division reports its maximum profit given this CR allocation plus a valuation of the allocated resources. Thereby the central unit extends its knowledge concerning profit as a function of allocated CR. A formal derivation of this mechanism is provided in Appendix C; we continue with a more precise description of the procedure.

We start our exposition with a block-angular LP problem that represents the planning problem, but contrary to earlier sections we use the symbols B_n and b for the common constraints as they will be decomposed in a different way.

$$
\begin{array}{ll}
\text{Maximize} & p_1 x_1 + \ldots + p_N x_N \\
\text{s.t.} & B_1 x_1 + \ldots + B_N x_N \leqslant b \\
& Q_1 x_1 \qquad\qquad\quad \leqslant q_1 \\
& \qquad\quad \ddots \qquad\quad \vdots \\
& \qquad\qquad Q_N x_N \leqslant q_N \\
& x_1, \ldots, x_N \geqslant 0
\end{array}
\tag{4.6}
$$

Problem (4.6) can be rewritten as follows:

$$
\begin{array}{ll}
\text{Maximize} & p_1 x_1 + \ldots + p_N x_N \\
\text{s.t.} & B_1 x_1 - b_1 \qquad\qquad\qquad \leqslant 0 \\
& Q_1 x_1 \qquad\qquad\qquad\quad \leqslant q_1 \\
& \qquad\quad \ddots \qquad\qquad\quad \vdots \\
& \qquad\qquad B_N x_N - b_n \leqslant 0 \\
& \qquad\qquad Q_N x_N \quad \leqslant q_n \\
& b_1 + \ldots \qquad + b_N = b \\
& x_1, \ldots, x_N \geqslant 0
\end{array}
\tag{4.7}
$$

In terms of the divisional organization underlying the LP problem (4.7), the central unit tries to allocate all available CR such that the sum of the divisional profits is maximized. So the central unit likes to know each division's profit $P_n(b_n)$ as a function of its CR portion b_n. However, due to its lack of divisional information the central unit cannot know the profit functions $P_n(b_n)$, $n=1,\ldots,N$, completely.

The idea is to solve (4.7) several times with different fixed values of b_n, say $\bar{b}_n$, where $\bar{b}_1 + \ldots + \bar{b}_N = b$. In a number of planning sessions the divisions solve problems of the form

$$\text{Maximize } p_n x_n$$
$$\text{s.t.} \qquad B_n x_n \leqslant \bar{b}_n$$
$$\qquad\qquad Q_n x_n \leqslant q_n$$
$$\qquad\qquad x_n \geqslant 0 \tag{4.8}$$

and report their profit $\hat{P}_n$ and a valuation $\hat{\rho}_n$ of CR portion $\bar{b}_n$ to the central unit. We assume that each $\bar{b}_n$ is such that (4.8) is feasible. Formally, optimal solution value $\hat{P}_n$ of (4.8) and an optimal dual variable $\hat{\rho}_n$ associated with constraints $B_n x_n \leqslant \bar{b}_n$ are reported. (More precisely, $\hat{\rho}_n$ is the ρ-part of a dual extreme point $(\hat{\rho}_n, \hat{\eta}_n)$ where the optimal solution value $\hat{P}_n$ is attained.)

From the reported divisional profit and the valuation of allocated CR the central unit can derive a linear function that approximates the divisional profit as a function of allocated resources:

$$P_n(b_n) \leqslant \hat{P}_n + \hat{\rho}_n (b_n - \bar{b}_n) \quad , \quad b_n \in U_n \tag{4.9}$$

Here U_n denotes the set of feasible CR allocations for division n.
By combining the divisional responses from all planning sessions up to 'now', i.e. an intermediate point in the planning process, a piecewise-linear approximation for each of these profit functions is obtained. Such a piecewise-linear function may, in a certain range, coincide with the real (but unknown) divisional profit function but will elsewhere majorize the real divisional profit function. Therefore, the optimization based on this partial information yields an optimistic 'estimate' of the divisional profit.

48

Together with the estimates of the divisional profits, say $\bar{P}_1,\ldots,\bar{P}_N$, the central unit computes the corresponding CR allocations $\bar{b}_1,\ldots,\bar{b}_N$. The optimality test is: can each division indeed realize the optimistic profit estimate, i.e. $\bar{P}_n$, if it obtains its portion $\bar{b}_n$? If the answer is 'yes' for all divisions, the planning procedure can be terminated. Otherwise, the divisions are also asked for a per-unit valuation $\hat{\rho}_n$ of the current CR portion $\bar{b}_n$. This information is used by the central unit, to improve the piecewise-linear approximation of the divisional profit function. Note that the total profit as 'estimated' by the central unit (i.e. $\bar{P}_1 + \ldots + \bar{P}_N$) is an upper bound of the actual (but still unknown) total profit. Moreover, the sequence of upper bounds as generated during the planning procedure is decreasing.

Altogether, the central unit provides for quantity-oriented information and the divisions respond with price-oriented information. So the nature of the information exchange is opposite to that of the price-directive procedure outlined earlier. See figure 4.3.

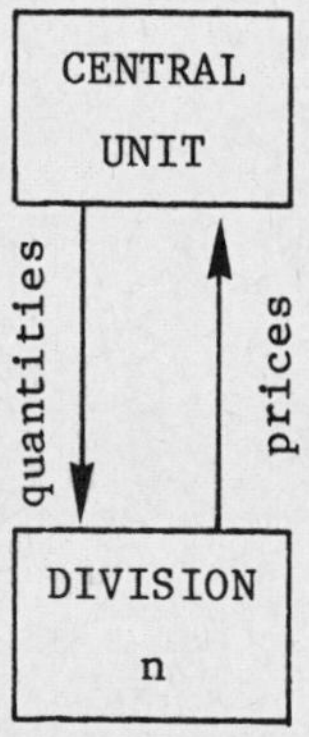

Figure 4.3: Information exchange in the resource-directive planning procedure according to Benders.

4.5. Discussion

Now that we have presented two decomposition-based planning procedures as illustrations of price-directive and resource-directive approaches, we will discuss the significance of these procedures as conceptual tools for analysing multilevel organizations. Furthermore, this section is devoted to a few related issues and features that are economically interesting.

It is evident that both procedures have multilevel characteristics as discussed in section 1.4. The overall planning problem is decomposed into a set of subproblems related and delegated to the sub-units in the company. Central unit as well as divisions actively participate in calculating the plan. However, the procedures adapt to relatively simple organizational structures:
1. there are only two hierarchical levels;
2. the information flows take place between the central unit and every division, not among the divisions, i.e. not within one hierarchical level.

Furthermore, the overall problem formulation is essentially static, so that only short-run planning problems can be considered.

Because of these limitations the practical applicability of such procedures as institutional planning devices in real-world organizations is probably limited. In the literature several simulation experiments with data from existing companies are reported on. Dirickx and Jennergren (1979, ch. 6 and section 11.2) review these test cases and conclude that the results are not really encouraging. In a later publication Burton and Obel (1980) provides quite a few general conclusions drawn from a simulation study. But we doubt whether their original overall model (i.e. a practical version of problem (4.1)) is representative enough to defend their generalizations and interpretations of the experimental outcomes.

The present study, however, serves more general purposes. The goal is to gain basic understanding of multilevel decision-making, in particular planning in decentralized firms. The analysis is of a descriptive, theoretical nature. Through the economic and organizational interpretation of decomposition methods, a useful conceptual framework is obtained that is straightforward, not too complicated, and that recognizes certain essential ingredients of a multilevel problem setting.

One of the strongest arguments in favour of decomposition-based planning procedures is the feature that these procedures can handle informational decentralization. In large organizations the necessary information for making decisions is localized in several parts of the organization, and planning procedures as outlined in sections 4.3 and 4.4 fit into various forms of this <u>information dispersal</u>.

As an example, consider the Dantzig-Wolfe method. The procedure can be applied if each division knows its production possibilities, in terms of the sets $\{x_n \mid O_n x_n \leqslant q_n, \ x_n \geqslant 0\}$, whereas the central unit knows the amounts of available CR, the vector a. The knowledge of A_n, the per-unit requirements for CR, and p_n, the per-unit contributions to the profit, can be located in various ways. It is allowed that
- the divisions do not know p_n and A_n, or
- the divisions do not know p_n, or
- the divisions know their own p_n and A_n.

Each of these situations gives rise to a different exchange of information between higher and lower levels. Combinations are also possible: for instance, some divisions know only their p_n, while the others know their A_n as well as their p_n. Formally, information dispersal can be defined as the specification of each subunit's knowledge of the constant coefficients of the entire planning problem.

The description of the planning procedure was almost entirely centred around the process of generating information from divisions until further planning cycles were not necessary anymore. In the sequel, the start of the planning process (initialization) and the computation of the final production plan (termination) will be discussed.

It is reasonable to expect that the central unit has some information on the divisions at the beginning of the planning procedure. This <u>a priori information</u> could have been derived from an earlier planning process, for instance from the final production plan of the previous year. Hence, the central unit has a priori 'feeling' for reasonable initial prices and CR allocations respectively. For instance in the Benders case, we implicitly assumed that some tentative CR allocation does not render divisional problem (4.8) infeasible. In other words, the central unit is assumed to know a priori which CR allocations are allowed from the divisional point of view; the central unit knows sets U_n, $n=1,\ldots,N$.

An interesting and valuable theoretical contribution concerning a priori information is provided by Frauendorfer (1984). This author discusses significant ranges for CR allocations, to be determined at the divisional level before the start of the planning procedure. Such ranges exclude a priori those divisional production plans which would cause infeasibility from a firm-wide point of view or which do not affect the firm-wide optimum. For completeness, we mention the publication by Burton and Obel (1980) discussed above, which also reports on the performance of planning procedures under various a priori information settings.

We conclude the evaluation of decomposition-based planning procedures with some thoughts on the statement of the final production plan to be obtained at the end of the planning phase. In the Benders case, we noted that the divisional production plans $\hat{x}_n$ in the final planning session, i.e. the divisional production plans given the latest CR allocations $\bar{b}_1,\ldots,\bar{b}_N$, are optimal for the firm as a whole. Therefore the final CR allocations can be applied as a coordinating instrument: they direct the divisions to optimal actions. On the other hand, the final divisional production plans in the Dantzig-Wolfe procedure need not be firm-wide optimal; they can be even globally infeasible. We will investigate this situation further.

Upon termination of the Dantzig-Wolfe procedure, a price π_0^{opt} for CR results under which the divisions cannot propose better production plans anymore. The firm-wide optimal production plan is some 'weighted average' of earlier divisional proposals. It would be practical if, given the termination price π_0^{opt}, each division chooses production plans according to the firm-wide optimum. So the question is: if divisions solve (4.3) with $\bar{\pi}_0$ equal to π_0^{opt}, is their local optimum also globally optimal? Baumol and Fabian (1964) have demonstrated that divisions may choose optima that do not coincide with the overall optimum. Geometrically, this remarkable feature can be clarified as follows: divisional optima always occur at a boundary point of the divisional feasible region, whereas the projection of the global optimum on a division's feasible region may well be an interior point (see also Lasdon (1970, pp. 162–163)). Summarizing, the final 14rice for CR, π_0^{opt}, does not coordinate the divisions in the sense of directing them to actions that are optimal for the company as a whole (see also Dirickx and Jennergren (1979, section 2.1, especially pp. 14–15). Mesarović et al. (1970) notes that it is the sequence of coordinating inputs (in our case, the $\bar{\pi}_0$ in every planning session) that leads to optimality, rather than one particular value of the coordination input (i.e. π_0^{opt}).

The computation of the firm-wide desired production plan thus cannot be accomplished through prices. Instead, the central unit can compute each globally optimal divisional production by using formula (4.5) with $\bar{\lambda}_n^i$ equal to final weights $(\lambda_n^i)^{opt}$, and then announce to each division its $\bar{x}_n$. However, this would leave a minimum degree of freedom to the divisions. A second method, that is less centralized and seems more appropriate in the given organizational structure, is to compute the divisions' ultimate portions of CR, i.e. $(n=1,\ldots,N)$

$$a_n^{opt} := \sum_{i=1}^{\bar{S}_n} (\lambda_n^i)^{opt} A_n^i, \tag{4.10}$$

and announce to each division its ultimate portion a_n^{opt}. Subsequently, each division solves problem (4.2) with a_n equal to a_n^{opt}, and in this way the computation of the detailed production plan is delegated to the divisions. It is evident that the divisional solutions are still firm-wide optimal.

Thus, with respect to the statement of the final production plan, we see that the actual decision concerning CR allocations is made at the top level in the organization. In other words, not so much decision authority is really delegated to divisions.

4.6. <u>Summary</u>

The conclusion of this chapter is that analysing decomposition-based planning procedures provides useful conceptual insight into multilevel planning situations. The procedures discussed in this chapter can be adapted to various forms of informational decentralization. On the other hand, the final decisions are still made at the top level in the organizations, so we have no decentralization of decision-making authority.

Before applying the gained insights to the general model of the firm as developed in chapters two and three, the next chapter treats more sophisticated procedures. Price and resource-directive characteristics are mixed and thus yield more realistic descriptions of planning processes.

CHAPTER FIVE

DECOMPOSITION BASED PLANNING:
MIXED PRICE-RESOURCE DIRECTIVE APPROACHES

5.1. Introduction

Usually a decomposition-based planning procedure is either price- or
resource-directive. This means that the coordination of subunits at the
lower level in the organization is accomplished by prices or by quantities. In real organizations, prices and direct resource allocations
often occur simultaneously as coordinating instruments. Therefore it is
interesting to investigate mixed price-resource directive decomposition
methods.

One way of mixing prices and quantities is division-oriented mixed
decomposition (DMD), where part of the divisions are coordinated by
prices while the remaining divisions are coordinated by resource allocation. For instance, manpower can be allocated to some divisions on the
basis of prices, where, at the same time, the other divisions are faced
with a budget for manpower, i.e. a direct allocation of manpower. The
second mixed approach is resource-oriented mixed decomposition (RMD).
Here a subset of the CR-types are coordinated by prices while the remaining CR-types are coordinated by direct allocations. Atkins (1973)
suggests that 'soft' common constraints may well be handled by price
coordination, (e.g. concerning resources that can be additionally
bought), whereas for 'hard' constraints direct coordination seems to be
more appropriate.

In the literature, mixed decomposition was introduced by Obel (1978),
who used the terms vertical and horizontal mixed decomposition, instead
of DMD and RMD respectively. Similar ideas, with emphasis on the economic implications, have been found in a working paper by Atkins (1979).

We will present a DMD and an RMD planning procedure (sections 5.2 and
5.3). Contrary to Obel (1978), substantial attention is paid to the res-
pective master problems, i.e the coordinating problems the central unit
is faced with. In the RMD case we follow the approach of an earlier
paper, viz. Meijboom (1985). Again, we will stress the economic significance of both methods as information gathering procedures.

5.2. <u>Division-oriented mixed decomposition</u>

In this section a hybrid version of the two planning procedures as presented in sections 4.3 and 4.4 is discussed. Certain divisions are coordinated by prices; the others are faced with direct resource allocations. Without loss of generality, the case with only two divisions is considered:

$$\text{Maximize } p_1 x_1 + p_2 x_2$$

$$\begin{aligned}
\text{s.t.} \quad A_1 x_1 + B_2 x_2 &\leqslant a \\
Q_1 x_1 &\leqslant q_1 \\
Q_2 x_2 &\leqslant q_2 \\
x_1, x_2 &\geqslant 0
\end{aligned} \tag{5.1}$$

A complete presentation of the procedure would be a mixture of sections 4.3 and 4.4. However, we leave this synthesis to the reader and provide a summary of the planning procedure. In brief, division 1 faces prices for CR and responds with plan proposals, while division 2 faces allocations of CR and responds with valuations. Based on the divisional responses the central unit decides upon continuation or termination of the planning procedure. See figure 5.1.

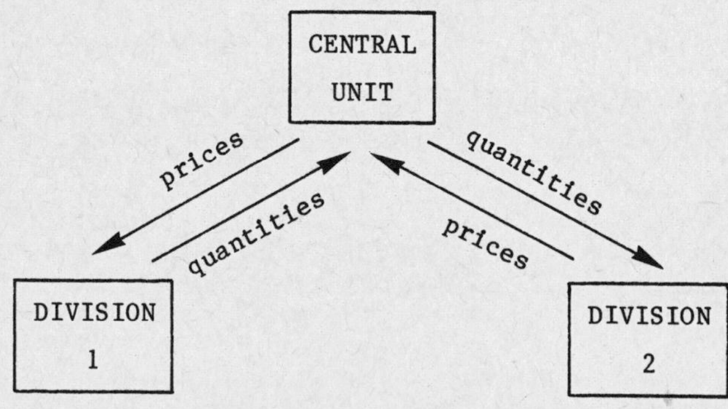

<u>Figure 5.1</u>: Information exchange in the DMD-based planning procedure.

At the beginning of each planning session, the central unit announces tentative prices $\bar{\pi}_0$ for CR to division 1 and a tentative allocation $\bar{b}_2$ of CR to division 2. Now division 1 has to solve

$$\text{Maximize } (p_1 - \bar{\pi}_0 A_1) x_1$$
$$\text{s.t.} \qquad Q_1 x_1 \leq q_1$$
$$x_1 \geq 0 \qquad\qquad (5.2)$$

and report the optimal production plan with associated profit to the central unit. At the same time, division 2 solves

$$\text{Maximize } p_2 x_2$$
$$\text{s.t.} \qquad B_2 x_2 \leq \bar{b}_2$$
$$Q_2 x_2 \leq q_2$$
$$x_2 \geq 0 \qquad\qquad (5.3)$$

and reports the maximal profit and a valuation of the allocated resources to the central unit.

In the course of the planning procedure, the central unit 'reveals' a number of production possibilities of division 1. At the same time, it gathers information concerning the profit of division 2 as a function of allocated CR. Hence, at each stage in the planning process the central unit has different types of information on the two divisions available. An obvious reason for mixing price- and resource-directive planning is the dispersal of information at the beginning of the planning procedure. The central unit's a priori knowledge on divisions may be such that it naturally chooses to coordinate one division by prices and the other by direct resource allocations.

Mathematical derivation of the procedure

The block-angular LP problem to be decomposed is given in (5.1). Matrices and vectors with index '1' will be decomposed according to Dantzig-Wolfe, and matrices and vectors with index '2' according to Benders.

Assume that the set $F_1 := \{x_1 \mid Q_1 x_1 \leq q_1, \, x_1 \geq 0\}$ is bounded. Problem (5.1) can be reformulated as follows:

58

$$\text{Maximize} \quad \sum_{i=1}^{S_1} p_1 x_1^i \lambda^i + P_2$$

$$\text{s.t.} \quad \sum_{i=1}^{S_1} A_1 x_1^i \lambda^i \qquad\qquad + b_2 = a$$

$$\sum_{i=1}^{S_1} \lambda^i \qquad\qquad\qquad = 1$$

$$P_2 - p_2 x_2 \quad\leqslant 0$$

$$B_2 x_2 - b_2 \leqslant 0$$

$$Q_2 x_2 \qquad \leqslant q_2$$

$$\text{all } \lambda^i \geqslant 0, \ x_2 \geqslant 0 \qquad\qquad (5.4)$$

Here x_1^i, $i=1,\ldots,S_1$, denote the extreme points of F_1. Now let (ρ_2^j, η_2^j), $j=1,\ldots,S_2$, be the extreme points of the dual region $\{(\rho_2,\eta_2) \mid \rho_2 B_2 + \eta_2 Q_2 \geqslant p_2; \ \rho_2, \ \eta_2 \geqslant 0\}$. Assuming that b_2 is chosen from the set $U_2 :=$ $\{b_2 \mid \exists_{x_2} (B_2 x_2 \leqslant b_2, Q_2 x_2 \leqslant q_2, x_2 \geqslant 0)\}$, problem (5.4) is equivalent to the following full master problem (FMP):

$$\text{Maximize} \quad \sum_{i=1}^{S_1} p_1 x_1^i \lambda^i + P_2$$

$$\text{s.t.} \quad \sum_{i=1}^{S_1} A_1 x_1^i \lambda^i \qquad + \quad b_2 = a$$

$$\sum_{i=1}^{S_1} \lambda^i \qquad\qquad = 1$$

$$P_2 - \rho_2^j b_2 \leqslant \eta_2^j q_2, \qquad j=1,\ldots,S_2$$

$$\text{all } \lambda^i \geqslant 0 \qquad\qquad (5.5)$$

The dual of the FMP, to be referred to as FMP-d, is:

$$\text{Minimize } \pi_0 a \quad + \pi_1 + \sum_{j=1}^{S_2} \mu^j \eta_2^j q_2$$

$$\text{s.t.} \quad \pi_0 A_1 x_1^i + \pi_1 \quad \geqslant p_1 x_1^i, \quad i=1,\dots,S_1$$

$$\sum_{j=1}^{S_2} \mu^j = 1$$

$$\pi_0 \quad - \sum_{j=1}^{S_2} \mu^j \rho_2^j = 0$$

$$\text{all } \mu^i \geqslant 0 \tag{5.6}$$

In each iteration, a restricted version of FMP is solved. This restricted master problem (RMP) takes into account some of the columns indexed by superscripts i and some of the rows indexed by superscript j. If we extend the solution to RMP by setting $\lambda^i = 0$ for every column i which has not been specified in RMP, we obtain a vector which does not violate the equality constraints of FMP. If we extend the solution to RMP-d by setting $\mu^j = 0$ for every row j which was not specified in RMP, we obtain a vector which does not violate the equality constraints of FMP-d.

Hence we can construct a primal and a dual solution, denoted by $(\bar{\lambda}^1,\dots,\bar{\lambda}^S 1, \bar{z}_2, \bar{b}_2)$ and $(\bar{\pi}_0, \bar{\pi}_1, \bar{\mu}^1,\dots,\bar{\mu}^S 2)$, respectively, which are 'partially feasible' to FMP and its dual, and the objective function values of which are equal to each other. If this primal-dual pair also satisfies the inequality constraints in FMP and as FMP-d, respectively, an optimum of FMP has been found. Therefore we must check whether

$$p_1 x_1^i - \bar{\pi}_0 A_1 x_1^i - \bar{\pi}_1 \leqslant 0, \quad i=1,\dots,S_1, \tag{5.7}$$

equivalent to

$$\max \left\{ (p_1 - \bar{\pi}_0 A_1) x_1 \mid Q_1 x_1 \leqslant q_1, \ x_1 \geqslant 0 \right\} \leqslant \bar{\pi}_1, \tag{5.8}$$

and

$$\bar{P}_2 \leqslant \rho_2^j \bar{b}_2 + \eta_2^j q_2, \quad j=1,\dots,S_2, \tag{5.9}$$

equivalent to

$$\bar{P}_2 \leqslant \min \left\{ \rho_2 \bar{b}_2 + \eta_2 q_2 \mid \rho_2 B_2 + \eta_2 Q_2 \geqslant P_2; \; \rho_2, \; \eta_2 \geqslant 0 \right\} \tag{5.10}$$

In case (5.8), the Dantzig-Wolfe criterion, is not fulfilled, a column is to be added to RMP. In case (5.10), the Benders criterion, is not fulfilled, a row is to be added to RMP. In both cases, RMP is then re-solved with an augmented set of columns and/or rows. As soon as (5.8) and (5.10) are fulfilled, optimality has been achieved and the procedure can be terminated.

5.3. Resource-oriented mixed decomposition

The present section is devoted to decomposable planning problems in which two sorts of common constraints are distinguished:

Maximize $p_1 x_1 + \ldots + p_N x_N$

$$
\begin{aligned}
\text{s.t.} \quad & A_1 x_1 + \ldots + A_N x_N \leqslant a && (*) \\
& B_1 x_1 + \ldots + B_N x_N \leqslant b && (**) \\
& Q_1 x_1 \qquad\qquad\quad \leqslant q_1 \\
& \qquad\qquad\qquad \vdots \\
& \qquad\quad Q_N x_N \leqslant q_N \\
& x_1, \ldots, x_N \geqslant 0 && (5.11)
\end{aligned}
$$

We will present a new two-level decomposition method (Meijboom (1985)) in which common constraints (*) are coordinated by prices while common constraints (**) are coordinated by direct allocations. This treatment of common constraints (*) and (**) will be referred to as resource-oriented mixed decomposition. Common constraints (*) and (**) are taken to express the common use of certain resources by all divisions. Firstly, the mathematical derivation of this new approach will be given. In this context we will speak of an algorithm rather than of a planning

procedure. Subsequently the economic implications are thoroughly analysed.

Before presenting the algorithm, a few assumptions and definitions are
in order. We assume the existence of a feasible solution of problem
(5.11). The divisional feasible regions F_n, which are defined as
$F_n := \{x_n | Q_n x_n \leqslant q_n, x_n \geqslant 0\}$ are assumed to be bounded. So (5.11) has a
finite optimum. For $n = 1,\ldots,N$, the set U_n is again defined as follows:

$$U_n := \{b_n \mid \text{a vector } x_n \in F_n \text{ exists with } B_n x_n \leqslant b_n\} \qquad (5.12)$$

Set U_n will be called the set of feasible allocations for division n
concerning common resources (**).

For notational convenience, set U is introduced:

$$U := \{(b_1,\ldots,b_N) \mid \sum_{n=1}^{N} b_n \leqslant b; \; b_n \in U_n, \; n = 1,\ldots, N\} \qquad (5.13)$$

Set U will be called the set of globally feasible allocations concerning
common resources (**).

5.3.1. <u>Development of the algorithm</u>

The Lagrange function relative to common constraints (*) is:

$$L(x,\pi) := \sum_{n=1}^{N} p_n x_n + \pi(a - \sum_{n=1}^{N} A_n x_n)$$

where x replaces $x_1,\ldots,x_N$. Now the (Lagrange) dual of (5.11) is:

$$\text{Min}_{\pi \geqslant 0} \; \text{Max}_{x} \; L(x,\pi)$$

$$\text{s.t. } x_n \in F_n, \; n=1,\ldots,N, \; \sum_{n=1}^{N} B_n x_n \leqslant b \qquad (5.14)$$

Optimal solutions $(\tilde{x},\tilde{\pi})$ to the minmax problem (5.14) are saddle points
of $L(x,\pi)$. The next theorem provides the necessary and sufficient conditions for the existence of a saddle point.

<u>Theorem 5.1:</u>

A vector $\tilde{x} = (\tilde{x}_1,\ldots, \tilde{x}_n)$ is a solution to the LP problem (5.9) if, and only if, a vector $\tilde{\pi} \geqslant 0$ exists such that $(\tilde{x},\tilde{\pi})$ is a saddle point of $L(x,\pi)$.

Proof: see Appendix D.

The usefulness of a saddle point is evident: if $(\tilde{x},\tilde{\pi})$ is a saddle point of $L(x,\pi)$, then $\tilde{x}$ solves the original problem (5.11).

If we use the set U (see formula (5.13)) and introduce functions $P_n(\pi,b_n)$ defined as

$$P_n(\pi,b_n) := \text{Max}\{(p_n-\pi A_n)x_n \mid x_n \in F_n,\ B_n x_n \leqslant b_n\},\ n = 1,\ldots,N,$$

problem (5.14) can be rewritten as

$$\underset{\pi \geqslant 0}{\text{Min}} \quad \underset{(b_1,\ldots,b_N)\,\in\,U}{\text{Max}} \quad \sum_{n=1}^{N} P_n(\pi,b_n) + \pi a \tag{5.15}$$

Problem (5.14) and (5.15) are equivalent because, for every $\pi \geqslant 0$, the inner maximization problems are equivalent (see Lasdon (1970, p. 462)). Functions $P_n(\pi,b_n)$ are concave in b_n and convex in π. Moreover, they are even piecewise-linear in both b_n and π.

Due to the assumed existence of a finite optimum of (5.11), the original Lagrangian $L(x,\pi)$ has a saddle point. So the function $\sum_{n=1}^{N} P_n(\pi,b_n) + \pi a$ has a saddle point, too. Hence, it is allowed to reverse the order of maximization and minimization in (5.15) (see Zangwill (1969, pp. 45-46), thereby obtaining:

$$\underset{(b_1,\ldots,b_N)\,\in\,U}{\text{Max}} \quad \underset{\pi \geqslant 0}{\text{Min}} \quad \sum_{n=1}^{N} P_n(\pi,b_n) + \pi a \tag{5.16}$$

In the sequel, (5.15) will be referred to as (D), the dual problem, and (5.16) as (P), the primal problem. Problems (P) and (D) have the same optimal solutions. Equivalent formulations of (P) and (D) are

$$\underset{(b_1,\ldots,b_N) \in U}{\text{Max}} \quad w \quad \text{s.t.} \quad w \leqslant \sum_{n=1}^{N} P_n(\pi,b_n) + \pi a, \quad \pi \geqslant 0 \qquad (5.17)$$

and

$$\underset{\pi \geqslant 0}{\text{Min}} \quad v \quad \text{s.t.} \quad v \geqslant \sum_{n=1}^{N} P_n(\pi,b_n) + \pi a, \quad (b_1,\ldots,b_N) \in U \qquad (5.18)$$

respectively. By applying tangential approximation, we will derive appropriate relaxed versions of (P) and (D).

Suppose we have at hand r sets $\{\pi^k, b_1^k, \ldots, b_N^k\}$, $k = 1,\ldots,r$, of tentative prices and allocations concerning common resources (*) and (**) respectively. Let $\pi^k \geqslant 0$, $b_n^k \in U_n$, $n=1,\ldots,N$, $\sum_{n=1}^{N} b_n^k \leqslant b$ for all k.

From $w \leqslant \sum_{n=1}^{N} P_n(\pi,b_n) + \pi a$, $\pi \geqslant 0$, it follows that

$$w \leqslant \sum_{n=1}^{N} P_n(\pi^k,b_n) + \pi^k a, \quad k = 1,\ldots,r \qquad (5.19)$$

Similarly

$$v \geqslant \sum_{n=1}^{N} P_n(\pi,b_n^k) + \pi a, \quad k = 1,\ldots,r \qquad (5.20)$$

The r right-hand sides of (5.19) are not easily handled, so we apply a further relaxation. Tangential approximations are readily obtained by solving the subproblems

$$\begin{aligned}
\text{Maximize} \quad & (p_n - \pi^k A_n)x_n \\
\text{s.t.} \quad & B_n x_n \leqslant b_n^k \\
& x_n \in F_n
\end{aligned} \qquad (5.21)$$

For, let $\hat{x}_n^k$ be an optimal solution, let $\hat{\rho}_n^k$ be an optimal dual solution associated with constraint $B_n x_n \leqslant b_n^k$, while the optimal solution value is $P_n(\pi^k,b_n^k)$ by definition. Then it is easy to show that

$$P_n(\pi^k, b_n) \leqslant P_n(\pi^k, b_n^k) + \hat{\rho}_n^k(b_n - b_n^k), \quad b_n \in U_n \tag{5.22}$$

(See Geoffrion (1970-a, p. 381) or Dirickx and Jennergren (1979, p. 69)). The right-hand sides of (5.20) can also be approximated:

$$\pi a + \sum_{n=1}^{N} P_n(\pi, b_n^k) \geqslant P_{sum}^k + (\pi - \pi^k) \Delta_a^k \tag{5.23}$$

where $(k = 1, \ldots, r)$:

$$P_{sum}^k := \sum_{n=1}^{N} P_n(\pi^k, b_n^k) + \pi^k a = \sum_{n=1}^{N} (p_n - \pi^k A_n)\hat{x}_n^k + \pi^k a,$$

$$\Delta_a^k := a - \sum_{n=1}^{N} A_n \hat{x}_n^k \tag{5.24}$$

(See Appendix D.)

Combining (5.17), (5.19) and (5.22) yields the following relaxed primal problem:

$$\text{Max} \quad w$$

$$\text{s.t.} \quad w \leqslant P_{sum}^k + \sum_{n=1}^{N} \hat{\rho}_n^k(b_n - b_n^k) \,, \quad k = 1, \ldots, r$$

$$(b_1, \ldots, b_N) \in U \tag{5.25}$$

From (5.18), (5.20) and (5.23), we derive the following relaxed dual problem:

$$\text{Min} \quad v$$

$$\text{s.t.} \quad v \geqslant P_{sum}^k + (\pi - \pi^k) \Delta_a^k \,, \quad k = 1, \ldots, r$$

$$\pi \geqslant 0 \tag{5.26}$$

Let $w(P)$ be the optimal solution value of (5.17), let $v(D)$ be the optimal solution value of (5.18). We know that $w(P) = v(D)$. Now, if w^r and v^r are the optimal solution values of (5.25) and (5.26) respectively, it holds that

$$v^r \leqslant v(D) = w(P) \leqslant w^r \tag{5.27}$$

So the optimal solution value of the original problem lies between v^r and w^r.

The algorithm approximates the solution of (P) and (D) by solving relaxed versions of (P) and (D), and adding new constraints to the relaxated problems when necessary.

Let $\varepsilon > 0$ be the desired accuracy. Suppose one has arrived at a relaxed primal and a relaxed dual problem of forms (5.25) and (5.26), respectively, each with r constraints. We call these problems (P_r) and (D_r). Solve (P_r) and denote the optimal solution by w^r, $b_1^{r+1}, \ldots, b_N^{r+1}$. Similarly, v^r and π^{r+1} denote the optimal solution to (D_r).

If $w^r - v^r < \varepsilon$, we may terminate. Now we can generate a globally feasible solution with value $\geqslant v^r$ (see section 5.3.2).

Otherwise, if $w^r - v^r \geqslant \varepsilon$, we solve the following subproblems:

$$
\begin{aligned}
\text{Max } & (p_n - \pi^{r+1} A_n) x_n \\
\text{s.t.} \quad & B_n x_n \leqslant b_n^{r+1} \\
& x_n \in F_n
\end{aligned}
\tag{5.28}
$$

This yields $\hat{x}_n^{r+1}$, $\hat{\rho}_n^{r+1}$, $P_n(\pi^{r+1}, b_n^{r+1})$, $n = 1, \ldots, N$, from which appropriate constraints to be added to (P_r) and (D_r) can be deduced. The augmented problems are called (P_{r+1}) and (D_{r+1}). If we solve (P_{r+1}) and (D_{r+1}), then w^{r+1} and v^{r+1} will result. These are, possibly better, upper/lower bounds for the optimal objective function value of the original problem as

$$v^r \leqslant v^{r+1} \leqslant v(D) = w(P) \leqslant w^{r+1} \leqslant w^r$$

Now it is clear that, by successively solving (P_r) and (D_r) and adding new constraints to them, we expect to find shrinking intervals $[v^r, w^r]$, $r = 1, 2, \ldots$, which contain the optimal objective function value. Indeed, the difference between v^r and w^r converges to zero. A convergence proof is given in Appendix D.

The algorithm can be summarized as follows:

Summary of algorithm:

Step 0. Choose $\pi^1 \geqslant 0$, and $b_n^1 \in U_n$, $n=1,\ldots,N$, such that $\sum\limits_{n=1}^{N} b_n^1 \leqslant b$. Set $r := 0$.

Step 1. For $n = 1,\ldots,N$, solve (5.28), which yields $\hat{x}_n^{r+1}$, $\hat{\rho}_n^{r+1}$ and $P_n(\pi^{r+1}, b_n^{r+1})$.

Step 2. Compute P_{sum}^{r+1} and Δ_a^{r+1}, and add appropriate constraints to (P_r) and (D_r) thereby obtaining (P_{r+1}) and (D_{r+1}), respectively.

Step 3. Set $r := r + 1$ and solve (P_r) and (D_r) which yields w^r, v^r, $b_1^{r+1},\ldots,b_N^{r+1}$, π^{r+1}.

Step 4. Optimality test:
if $w^r - v^r < \varepsilon$ then terminate, otherwise return to step 1.

Until now, we have treated set U as if it is completely known. In practical applications it is usually impossible to obtain set U (or the sets $U_1,\ldots,U_N$) in an explicit form. The literature, in particular Geoffrion (1970, section 3.1), offers several useful methods to generate sets $U_1,\ldots,U_N$ during the iterations of the algorithm described above. Especially in the present linear case, each U_n can be specified without approximation by a finite collection of linear equalities. Each of these inequalities can be added to (5.25) 'when needed'.

Secondly, sets $U_1,\ldots,U_N$ are partly determined by matrices $B_1,\ldots,B_N$ (cf. definition (5.12)). These matrices, in turn, depend on the choice between price-directive or resource-directive coordination for each of the common constraints. Note that these choices are to be made before actually starting the algorithm.

These aspects highlight the importance of the algorithm as an information gathering procedure.

5.3.2. <u>Generation of globally feasible solutions</u>

So far we described a procedure which simultaneously generates a decreasing sequence of upper bounds as well as an increasing sequence of lower bounds for the optimal solution value. Moreover, both sequences, i.e. $(v^r)_1^\infty$ and $(w^r)_1^\infty$, converge to this value. In this section, we will show that, without much extra effort, a globally feasible solution can be computed.

The relaxed dual (D_r) is simply an LP problem and can be written as

Minimize v

$$
\text{s.t.} \quad v - \pi \Delta_a^k \geqslant P_{sum}^k - \pi^k \Delta_a^k, \quad k = 1,\ldots,r
$$
$$
\pi \geqslant 0 \tag{5.29}
$$

Dualization yields:

$$
\text{Maximize} \quad \sum_{k=1}^{r} \lambda^k (P_{sum}^k - \pi^k \Delta_a^k)
$$

$$
\text{s.t.} \quad \sum_{k=1}^{r} \lambda^k = 1
$$

$$
- \sum_{k=1}^{r} \lambda^k \Delta_a^k \leqslant 0
$$
$$
\text{all } \lambda^k \geqslant 0 \tag{5.30}
$$

which is equivalent to (cf. (5.24)):

$$
\text{Maximize} \quad \sum_{k=1}^{r} \lambda^k \sum_{n=1}^{N} p_n \hat{x}_n^k
$$

$$
\text{s.t.} \quad \sum_{k=1}^{r} \lambda^k = 1
$$

$$
\sum_{k=1}^{r} \lambda^k \sum_{n=1}^{N} A_n \hat{x}_n^k \leqslant a
$$
$$
\text{all } \lambda^k \geqslant 0 \tag{5.31}
$$

Now let $(\bar{\lambda}^1,\ldots,\bar{\lambda}^r)$ be an optimal solution to (5.31). Its solution value is equal to v^r, the optimal value of (D_r). If we define

$$\bar{x}_n := \sum_{k=1}^{r} \bar{\lambda}^k \, \hat{x}_n^k, \qquad n = 1,\ldots,N \tag{5.32}$$

then $(\bar{x}_1,\ldots,\bar{x}_N)$ is feasible to (5.11), due to the convexity properties, and it has solution value v^r.

Summarizing we can derive a globally feasible solution by a convex combination of previously generated divisional solutions. The weighting factors are exactly the optimal dual variables associated with (D_r), and the solution value is equal to the optimal value of (D_r).

5.3.3. Economic interpretation

As noted before, the original problem (5.11) is viewed as the overall planning problem in a divisionalized organization. Blocks $Q_n x_n \leqslant q_n$, $x_n \geqslant 0$ $(n=1,\ldots,N)$ are associated with divisions and the common constraints (*) and (**) reflect the interdependencies between them (e.g. allocation of common resources). Furthermore, there is a central unit at the top level of the organization, that is aware of these interdependencies but does not have complete information on the divisional constraints. Therefore, a planning procedure by which top management gathers information, must be applied. Below we describe a procedure that is based on the decomposition algorithm as developed in section 5.3.1. The essential feature of the method is that
- the (*) interdependencies are coordinated by prices, while
- the (**) interdependencies are coordinated by direct allocations.
Hence, we provide a mixed price–resource directive planning procedure.

Recall that the (*) and (**) interdependencies are assumed to reflect the common use of certain resources by all divisions. The goal of the firm is assumed to be profit maximization.

The planning procedure is formed by a number of planning sessions. At the start of a new planning session, the central unit announces a tentative price π^r for the (*) resources and tentative direct allocations $b_1^r,\ldots,b_N^r$ of the (**) resources to the divisions. These are asked to compute their maximum profit $P_n(\pi^r, b_n^r)$, the required amount $A_n \hat{x}_n^r$ of (*) resources, and per-unit valuations $\hat{\rho}_n^r$ $(n=1,\ldots,N)$ of allocated (**) resources given price π^r and allocation $b_1^r,\ldots,b_N^r$. This information exchange is illustrated in figure 5.2.

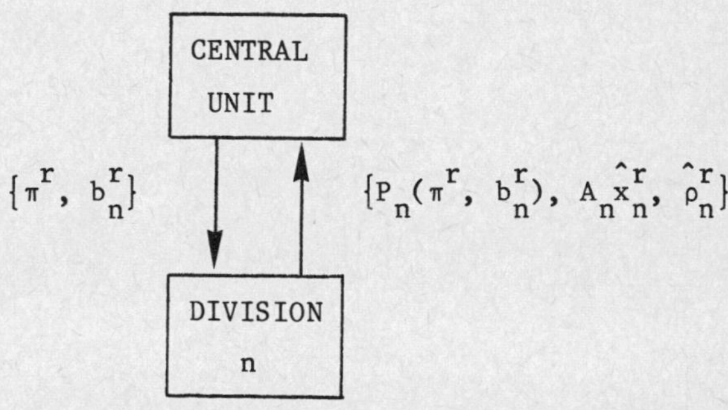

Figure 5.2: Information exchange in the r-th planning session of the RMD-based planning procedure.

Formally, each division solves its problem

$$\text{Maximize } (p_n - \pi^r A_n) x_n$$
$$\text{s.t.} \qquad B_n x_n \leqslant b_n^r$$
$$x_n \in F_n \qquad\qquad\qquad (5.33)$$

and reports optimal solution value $P_n(\pi^r, b_n^r)$, quantity $A_n \hat{x}_n^r$, where $\hat{x}_n^r$ is the optimal solution to (5.33), and an optimal dual variable $\hat{\rho}_n^r$ with respect to constraint $B_n x_n \leqslant b_n^r$.

Based on the divisional responses and on information gathered in previous sessions, the central unit can derive a lower bound v^r and an upper bound w^r for the maximum attainable total profit (i.e. the optimal value of the original problem (5.11)). The maximum attainable profit lies between these bounds, so the central unit can terminate the procedure as soon as the difference between lower and upper bound has become small enough. The central unit finds a distribution of the (*) and (**) resources at which the divisions together will at least realize a profit of v^r, if the previous claims for (*) resources, i.e. $A_n \hat{x}_n^k$, $k=1,\ldots,r$, and allocations of (**) resources, i.e. b_n^k, $k=1,\ldots,r$, are adequately weighted. Weighting factors with this property, which apply to both CR-types and are uniform over the divisions, can be obtained by a slight modification of the computational procedure for v^r.

Formally, the dual optimum to problem (D_r) delivers the desired weighting factors $\bar{\lambda}^1,\ldots,\bar{\lambda}^r$ (cf. section 5.3.2). Additionally the central unit must compute $(n=1,\ldots,N)$:

$$\bar{a}_n^r := \sum_{k=1}^r \bar{\lambda}^k A_n \hat{x}_n^k; \quad \bar{b}_n^r := \sum_{k=1}^r \bar{\lambda}^k b_n^k. \tag{5.34}$$

If the divisions optimally use these (final) amounts of CR, they solve the problems $(n=1,\ldots,N)$:

$$
\begin{aligned}
\text{Maximize } & p_n x_n \\
\text{s.t.} \quad & A_n x_n \leq \bar{a}_n^r \\
& B_n x_n \leq \bar{b}_n^r \\
& x_n \in F_n
\end{aligned}
\tag{5.35}
$$

and the sum of their profits will be at least v^r.

On the other hand, if the central unit is not satisfied with bounds v^r and w^r, it can update the prices and resource allocations leading to new bounds v^{r+1} and w^{r+1}. It will hold that

$$v^r \leq v^{r+1} \leq OPT \leq w^{r+1} \leq w^r \tag{5.36}$$

where OPT denotes the maximum attainable total profit. So the more information the central unit gathers, the better it approximates the maximum attainable profit.

Now we will pay attention to the way the central unit derives the prices, CR allocations and profit 'estimates' in subsequent planning sessions. To this end, we have to explain the economic meaning of problems (P) and (D), to be referred to as 'maxmin' and 'minmax' respectively.

For some fixed allocation of (**) resources, say $(\bar{b}_1,\ldots,\bar{b}_N) \in U$, the inner minimization of maxmin yields a price for (*) resources that minimizes the valuation of these resources given allocation $(\bar{b}_1,\ldots,\bar{b}_N)$. Hence maxmin determines an allocation of (**) resources that maximizes this valuation, i.e. the amount of money that the divisions together offer for (*) resources.

For some fixed price vector for (*) resources, say $\bar{\pi} \geqslant 0$, the inner maximization of minmax determines an allocation of (**) resources at which the divisions together maximize their total profit given price $\bar{\pi}$. Now minmax chooses a price for (*) resources that minimizes this total profit. So minmax determines the minimal valuation of (*) resources.

We know that maxmin and minmax have equal optimal solution values. This means: a price π^{opt} and an allocation $b_1^{opt},\ldots,b_N^{opt}$ exist at which the divisions together offer an amount of money for (*) resources exactly equal to the amount the central unit wants to receive minimally for these resources.

However, in the planning procedure the central unit is merely concerned with a 'pessimistic' version of (D) and with an 'optimistic' version of (P). As a result, the prices π^r and the lower bounds v^r on the one hand, and the allocations $b_1^r,\ldots,b_N^r$ and the upper bounds w^r on the other follow from two separate computations. We will first consider the prices π^r together with the lower bounds v^r.

Suppose we are at the end of the r-th planning session. The central unit has at hand the divisional responses of sessions $1,2,\ldots,r$. From the divisional responses of each session separately, the central unit can form a linear function which approximates the maximal profit of the divisions together as a function of the internal prices π. Hence, combining the divisional information as collected in all previous sessions up to this moment, the central unit derives a piecewise-linear approximation of this profit as a function of the prices for (*) resources. The collected information is used in a 'pessimistic' way, since the approximating valuation function lies below the correct profit function. The estimated minimal valuation of (*) resources v^r is exactly the minimum value of this approximating function. As a result v^r is a lower bound for the correct minimal valuation. In the course of the procedure, the piecewise-linear approximating function becomes better and better, hence giving rise to improved lower bounds v^{r+1}, v^{r+2} etc.

The determination of subsequent w^r and $b_1^r,\ldots,b_N^r$ proceeds in a similar way. The difference is that here the central unit works with an improving piecewise-linear approximation for the minimal valuation of (*) resources as a function of the allocation of (**) resources, which always lies above the correct valuation function. Hence a decreasing sequence of upper bounds w^r is the result.

To conclude, we compare the present planning procedure with the two procedures of chapter four, that were based on the Dantzig-Wolfe and the Benders method.

Just like in the Benders case the updating of CR allocations is coupled with the generation of a decreasing sequence of optimistic profit estimates. And the price corrections are coupled with the generation of an increasing sequence of pessimistic profit estimates, similar to the Dantzig-Wolfe procedure.

Finally, we note that subproblem (5.21) (or (5.33)) is clearly a mixed version of problems (4.3) and (4.8) in chapter four.

5.4. Summary

The main purpose of this chapter has been to discuss two-level planning procedures with prices and direct allocations for resources occurring simultaneously. We were particularly interested in the computation of prices and allocations. In the RMD case, this computation provided an upper and lower bound for the optimal value of the problem at hand. The lower bound, which increases during the iteration sequence (cf. (5.36)), is directly associated with a globally feasible solution, so that globally feasible solutions can be obtained with increasing solution value. In the DMD case, monotonic bounds are not available.

The contribution of the present chapter is that it provides the correct mathematical foundation of mixed coordination by prices and budgets in a general two-level organization. Each of the subproblems, at the top level as well as at the divisional level, has a clear appealing economic interpretation in terms of a planning procedure. Secondly, the mixed use of prices and budgets is a most realistic feature when comparing the present planning procedure with planning in real-world organizations (e.g. see Atkins (1973), Obel (1981)). From a computational point of view, several improving modifications could be incorporated. However this is beyond the scope of the text.

CHAPTER SIX

OVERALL ANALYSIS OF THE MODEL OF THE FIRM

6.1. <u>Introduction</u>

In chapter two and three we have developed a general model of the firm, thus providing the economic context for our analysis of two-level planning. We included multiple techniques, make-or-buy decisions and cost allocation issues. Furthermore, a two-level organizational structure was proposed, with a central unit at the top level and a number of divisions at a lower level. The central unit's task is to coordinate the divisional consumption of common resources (CR), to determine the make-or-buy decisions for technical services (TS) and to allocate costs.

The problem of finding a firm-wide optimal technology and TS alternative without overconsumption of CR has been formulated as a mixed-integer programming (MIP) problem (see table 6.1). Provided a full specification of the constant coefficients in the MIP formulation is available, the solution can in principle be determined immediately. Subsequently, the common costs and the costs of internally produced TS are to be allocated by the central unit.

The present chapter is mainly devoted to the fictitious outcome of applying an appropriate overall solution technique to a fully specified version of the MIP problem. We will investigate the properties of optimal solutions. In fact the MIP model of the firm is analysed from an 'overall' point of view: the organizational aspects are neglected and the firm is considered as an entity directed by or identified with one single decision-maker who is 'all-knowing' and 'all-mighty'. In discussing the properties of the optimal solution to the MIP problem in terms of make-or-buy decisions, choice of techniques and CR consumption, we will keep these rather centralized circumstances in mind.

The overall approach leads to some insight in the relationships between production techniques and make-or-buy decisions. Secondly, the properties of the solution as obtained by the overall approach can func-

Maximize	$-c_1x_1 - dy_1 + p_1z_1$	$-c_2x_2 - dy_2 + p_2z_2$	$\cdots$	$-c_Nx_N - dy_N + p_Nz_N$		$-c_0x_0 - dy_0 - C\delta$
s.t.	A_1x_1	$+ A_2x_2$		$+ A_Nx_N$		$\leq a$
	$B_1x_1 - y_1$				$- b_1$	≤ 0
	$(I_1 - D_1)x_1 - z_1$					$= 0$
	z_1					$\leq f_1$
		$B_2x_2 - y_2$			$- b_2$	≤ 0
		$(I_2 - D_2)x_2 - z_2$				$= 0$
		z_2				$\leq f_2$
			$\ddots$			$\cdot$
				$B_Nx_N - y_N$	$- b_N$	≤ 0
				$(I_N - D_N)x_N - z_N$		$= 0$
				z_N		$\leq f_N$
					$b_1 + b_2 \cdots + b_N - b_0$	$= 0$
					$b_0 - (I - D_0)x_0 - y_0$	$= 0$
					b_0	$- W\delta \leq 0$
					x_0	$- W\delta \leq 0$

all x_n, y_n, z_n, $b_n \geq 0$

δ : 0-1 vector

W : large positive constant

Table 6.1: Problem (6.1): the MIP formulation of the two-level divisionalized firm.

tion as a reference when we, subsequently, investigate the properties of
the solution under more decentralized circumstances.

The chapter is organized as follows. First properties of overall solutions are treated (section 6.2) followed by a numerical example that
informally clarifies obtained results (section 6.3). Then the establishment of an overall plan is discussed (section 6.4). Finally cost allocation mechanisms are proposed (section 6.5).

6.2. <u>Properties of overall solutions</u>

In this section we consider the MIP formulation of the general model of
the firm as a computational problem with all input data available and
thus immediately solvable. Recall that the MIP problem integrates all
possible technology and TS-alternatives in one overall formulation. Here
a technology alternative is a collection of techniques at least one for
each product, and a TS alternative is a combination of make-or-buy decisions stating which TS types are produced internally and which TS types
are bought externally. The outcome of the overall solution approach will
be referred to as the <u>overall solution</u>. It implies a technology alternative and a TS alternative which are optimal from a firm-wide point of
view. From the overall solution the CR and internal-TS portions of each
division, denoted by a_n^{opt} and b_n^{opt} respectively, can be derived.

As an intermediate step, we will analyse the overall solution for a
situation with omission of the CR constraints, as if each CR is available in unlimited amounts. Subsequently, we turn to the general case in
which each CR-type is available in limited amounts. Two useful theorems
are presented. The formal proof is provided in Appendix E because it is
rather technical. The result will be explained from an economic point of
view.

6.2.1. <u>The case with common resources in excess supply</u>

Suppose CR is available in unlimited amounts. In these circumstances the
CR constraints can be omitted from the MIP problem. The resulting formulation does not differ essentially from the MIP model as presented at

the end of chapter two, i.e. problem (2.8). We will now compare problem (2.8) and problem (6.1) ignoring the CR constraints, and show that both problems must have optimal solutions of the same character.

The first difference between the two MIP models is that in table 6.1 products with directly interrelated production processes are grouped in divisions. So in comparison with (2.8) rows and columns are simply put in a specific order, which, in turn, does not affect the feasibility or even the optimality of the solutions. The other difference is the occurrence of a few additional constraints, namely $b_0 - W\delta \leqslant 0$, in problem (6.1). These constraints together with the non-negativity conditions $b_0, b_1, \ldots, b_N \geqslant 0$ rather guarantee that each division buys its external TS on its own, than affect choice of techniques, amounts of sold products or make-or-buy decisions. As a result, the following theorem is valid:

Theorem 6.1:

If the MIP problem as presented in table 6.1 with omission of the CR constraints has an optimum, then an optimal solution exists with the following properties:

1. For each product that is produced exactly one technique is applied.
2. Products are either sold maximally or not sold at all.
3. Each TS-type that is required is either produced internally or bought externally.

Proof: See Appendix E.

Just as in section 2.5, the variable part of the TS costs, given a particular TS alternative, can be regarded as direct costs. Given the (modified) direct costs of each of the production techniques, a pure technology alternative exists that can realize every final output at minimal costs. The per-unit redistributed variable costs given this technology alternative must be compared with the sales prices in order to determine which market products are 'profitable' and which are not, given the TS alternative. Of course, profitable products should be sold as many as possible, whereas unprofitable products should not be sold at all.

6.2.2. <u>The case with common resources in limited supply</u>

Now we turn to the case in which each of the CR is available in limited amounts. Contrary to the previous case, in which all CR was in excess supply, it is possible that products are sold on the outside market but below the outside demand level. Furthermore, an overall solution may exist that uses two or more techniques for a particular product. However, there are no overall solutions in which some TS-type is produced internally but also additionally bought from outside the company. We will first provide an economic clarification concerning the conjectures just mentioned.

Consider again the case without CR and suppose that there is a number of profitable product types given the optimal technology and TS-alternative. Profitable products should of course be sold as much as possible and unprofitable product types should not be sold; they only support the production of other products. The higher the outside demand for profitable products, the more of these product types the firm tries to sell. As a result, the entire production intensity, i.e. the production levels of profitable and unprofitable products, will increase. Returning to the situation including CR available in limited amounts, the main observation is that scarcity of one or more resources may limit the production level of products. This, in turn, affects the sales levels. So the presence of production constraints, due to the common use of certain resources, may force the management of the firm to sell profitable products below their outside demand level thereby receiving smaller revenues. However, there is a possibility to avoid these decreased sales levels.

For each product more than one production technique may exist. When faced with production volume barriers, the firm could try to apply different techniques for some products in order to reduce CR consumption. For instance, given the TS alternative of the preceding paragraph, suppose a technology alternative exists that can realize the outside demand for certain products while using less CR than available and still yielding a positive total profit P_{alt}. Denoting the total net profit of the case without CR by P_{orig}, it holds that $P_{alt} < P_{orig}$. In order to improve P_{alt}, the firm will now mix the corresponding CR-extensive production and sales schedule with the original P_{orig} yielding schedule such that the CR are precisely used up. The ultimate profit P_{mix} will lie between P_{alt} and P_{orig}, i.e. $P_{alt} \leqslant P_{mix} \leqslant P_{orig}$, and for at least one product type two or more techniques are applied.

Now we present the formal result with respect to mixed techniques and lowered sales levels. Recall that Φ_n denotes the number of product types in division n and L denotes the number of CR-types.

Theorem 6.2:

Let δ^{opt} be part of an optimal solution to problem (6.1). Assume that the optimum of the continuous LP problem that is obtained if δ is taken equal to δ^{opt} is unique. For this optimum:

1. we assume that each TS-type is required while in every division every product is produced;

2. we define μ_n, β_n, SA as follows:

   μ_n := the number of techniques as applied in division n (n=1,...,N);

   β_n := the number of product types in division n that are sold but below the outside demand level, so $0 \leqslant \beta_n \leqslant \Phi_n$ (n=1,...,N);

   SA := the number of CR-types that are not fully used up, so

   $0 \leqslant SA \leqslant L$.

Then it holds that:

$$\mu_n - \Phi_n \geqslant 0, \ n=1,...,N, \qquad (6.2\text{-}a)$$

$$0 \leqslant \sum_{n=1}^{N} ((\mu_n - \Phi_n) + \beta_n) \leqslant L - SA. \qquad (6.2\text{-}b)$$

Furthermore each TS-type is either produced internally or bought externally.

Proof: The result is proved in Appendix E.

Suppose part of the CR-types are not fully used up so that $0 < SA < L$ and thus $L - SA > 0$. Then formula (6.2-b) implies that, for at least one n, we have $\mu_n - \Phi_n > 0$ or $\beta_n > 0$. In other words, at least one division exists that applies more than the minimum number of Φ_n techniques (so that for at least one product two or more techniques are applied), or that sells at least one of its product below the outside demand level. So under the stated assumptions we have demonstrated that 'mixing' and/ or 'decreased sales levels' indeed occur. However, the above theorem does not provide information concerning the number of applied techniques per product.

6.3. Numerical example

The overall analysis as provided in the preceding sections yields several formalized general results. For instance Theorems 6.1 and 6.2 summarize general properties concerning mixed techniques, decreased sales levels and TS alternatives in a more or less formal way. In this section we will present a numerical example that is meant as an informal clarification of obtained results. The data of the example are not borrowed from an existing planning problem: we work with a low-dimension instance of problem (6.1) which has been constructed for the purpose of illustration.

Description of the example

In terms of the general model of the firm (cf. section 3.5) we have at hand a fictitious enterprise with two divisions: $N=2$. Each division produces two different product types, so $\Phi_n = 2$ $(n=1,2)$. In division 1, the first product type, i.e. $X_{1,1}$, can be produced in two alternative ways, while the second product type, i.e. $X_{1,2}$, has just one single production technique: $\Psi_{1,1} = 2$, $\Psi_{1,2} = 1$. Similarly we have $\Psi_{2,1} = 2$, $\Psi_{2,2} = 1$ for division 2.

For the production in division 1 and 2, CR and TS are required. There are two CR types: $L=2$. There are three TS types: $M=3$. Division 1 asks for TS_1 and TS_3, division 2 asks for TS_2 and TS_3, and TS_1, TS_2, TS_3 also support each other, if they are produced internally.

In table 6.2 the data of the numerical example are provided.

__Table 6.2:__ Data of the numerical example.

__Product Divisions__

division	1			2		
product type	$X_{1,1}$	$X_{1,2}$		$X_{2,1}$	$X_{2,2}$	
sales prices	$P_1 = \quad (1000$	$, 1000)$		$P_2 = \quad (1000$	$, 1000)$	
outside demand	$f_1 = \quad (\;18$	$, 12)$		$f_2 = \quad (\;30$	$, 15)$	
technique	1	2	1	1	2	1
direct costs	$c_1 = (\;62$	$, 58$	$, 50)$	$c_2 = (\;70$	$, 53.5$	$, 70)$
CR requirements	$A_1 = \begin{bmatrix} 1 & 1 & 0 \\ 2 & 1 & 0 \end{bmatrix} \begin{smallmatrix}\uparrow\\\downarrow\end{smallmatrix} L$			$A_2 = \begin{bmatrix} 0.5 & 1 & 0 \\ 0.5 & 0.25 & 0 \end{bmatrix} \begin{smallmatrix}\uparrow\\\downarrow\end{smallmatrix} L$		
TS requirements	$B_1 = \begin{bmatrix} 1.773 & 1.622 & 0 \\ 0 & 0 & 0 \\ 1.091 & 0.901 & 0 \end{bmatrix} \begin{smallmatrix}\uparrow\\ \\\downarrow\end{smallmatrix} M$			$B_1 = \begin{bmatrix} 0 & 0 & 0 \\ 1.167 & 1.33 & 0 \\ 1.083 & 1 & 0 \end{bmatrix} \begin{smallmatrix}\uparrow\\ \\\downarrow\end{smallmatrix} M$		
production	$I_1 - W_1 = \begin{bmatrix} 0.8 & 0.8 & -0.3 \\ 0.6 & -0.7 & 0.9 \end{bmatrix} \begin{smallmatrix}\uparrow\\\downarrow\end{smallmatrix} \Phi_1$			$I_2 - W_2 = \begin{bmatrix} 0.875 & 0.875 & -0.375 \\ -0.5 & -0.5 & 0.75 \end{bmatrix} \begin{smallmatrix}\uparrow\\\downarrow\end{smallmatrix} \Phi_2$		
number of techniques	$\xleftrightarrow{\hspace{2cm}} \Psi_{1,1} \quad \xleftrightarrow{} \Psi_{1,2}$			$\xleftrightarrow{\hspace{2cm}} \Psi_{2,1} \quad \xleftrightarrow{} \Psi_{2,2}$		

__TS sector__

input coefficients of internal TS production	$D_0 = \begin{bmatrix} 0 & 0.1667 & 0.5 \\ 0.333 & 0 & 0.1 \\ 0 & 0.04167 & 0 \end{bmatrix}$
per-unit direct costs	$c_0 = (\;80 \qquad , \quad 40 \qquad , \quad 24)$
fixed costs	$C = (6000 \qquad , 7000 \qquad , 2000)$
external TS prices	$d = (\;165 \qquad , \quad 195 \qquad , \quad 65)$
	$\xleftrightarrow{\hspace{4cm}} M$

the large positive constant W in problem (6.1) is taken equal to 200

Table 6.3: Overall solutions given four different CR-capacity vectors: total profit, divisional part and TS part respectively.

common resources		type		unlimited		$a=(60,80)$		$a=(80,60)$		$a=(80,30)$	
available	1	$a(1)$		unlimited		60		80		80	
	2	$a(2)$		unlimited		80		60		30	
used up	1			68.82		60		80		75	
	2			53.82		80		60		30	
TOTAL PROFIT				34517.27		32603.35		33882.13		30558.53	
DIVISIONS $n=1,2$				$n=1$	$n=2$	$n=1$	$n=2$	$n=1$	$n=2$	$n=1$	$n=2$
product type	technique	production volume									
1	1	$x_{n,1}(1)$		0	0	20	60	0	33.33	0	0
	2	$x_{n,1}(2)$		38.82	60	10	0	36.67	26.67	15	60
2	1	$x_{n,2}(1)$		43.52	60	34.44	60	41.85	60	25	60
product type	sales level										
1		$z_n(1)$		18	30	13.67	30	16.78	30	4.5	30
2		$z_n(2)$		12	15	12	15	12	15	12	15
TS type	external purchase										
1		$y_n(1)$		63	0	51.68	0	59.49	0	24.34	0
2		$y_n(2)$		0	0	0	0	0	0	0	0
3		$y_n(3)$		0	0	0	0	0	0	13.52	60
TS type	internal supply										
1		$b_n(1)$		0	0	0	0	0	0	0	0
2		$b_n(2)$		0	80	0	70	0	74.46	0	80
3		$b_n(3)$		35	60	30.83	65	33.05	62.78	0	0

	available CR unlimited			available CR $a=(60,80)$			available CR $a=(80,60)$			available CR $a=(80,30)$		
TS SECTOR $m=1,2,3$	$m=1$	$m=2$	$m=3$	$m=1$	$m=2$	$m=3$	$m=1$	$m=2$	$m=3$	$m=1$	$m=2$	$m=3$
TS alternative	0	1	1	0	1	1	0	1	1	0	1	0
internal production x_0	0	89.87	98.74	0	79.94	99.15	0	84.39	99.34	0	80	0
external purchase y_0	19.92	0	0	18.28	0	0	19.03	0	0	13.36	0	3.33
supply to divisions b_0	0	80	95	0	70	95.83	0	74.46	95.83	0	80	0

Overall solution for several CR capacities

In table 6.3 the results of solving the MIP example are presented given four different capacities for CR. First we optimize a version of the MIP example with omission of the CR constraints, as if CR are available in unlimited quantities. Note that:

1. $x_{1,1}(1) = 0$, $x_{1,1}(2) > 0$ so product type $X_{1,1}$ applies only one technique (viz. its second technique), and $x_{2,1}(1) = 0$, $x_{2,1}(2) > 0$ so product type $X_{2,1}$ applies just one technique.

2. $z_1 = (18,12) = f_1$, $z_2 = (30,15) = f_2$, i.e. all product types are sold maximally.

3. $x_0(1) = 0$, $y_0(1) > 0$, $y_1(1) > 0$ and $x_0(m) > 0$, $y_0(m) = 0$, $y_n(m) = 0$ for m=2,3. Hence each TS-type is either produced internally or bought externally.

Subsequently, the MIP example including the CR constraints is optimized with three different values of the CR-capacity vector $a = (a(1),a(2))$. The results can also be found in table 6.3.

- Case $a(1) = 60$, $a(2) = 80$:

  In division 1 product type $X_{1,1}$ is not sold maximally ($f_1(1) = 13.67 <$ 18) and applies both of its two techniques ($x_{1,1}(1) > 0$, $x_{1,1}(2) > 0$). In division 2 product type $X_{2,1}$ applies only its first technique ($x_{2,1}(1) > 0$, $x_{2,1}(2) = 0$). Both CR-types are fully used up.

- Case $a(1) = 80$, $a(2) = 60$:

  In division 1 product type $X_{1,1}$ is not sold maximally ($f_1(1) = 16,78 <$ 18). In division 2 product type $X_{2,1}$ applies both of its two techniques ($x_{2,1}(1) > 0$ and $x_{2,1}(2) > 0$). Both CR-types are fully used up.

- Case $a(1) = 80$, $a(2) = 30$:

  In division 1 product type $X_{1,1}$ is not sold maximally ($f_1(1) = 4.5 <$ 18). One CR-type is not fully used up. Note that in comparison with the two earlier cases TS_3 is not produced internally anymore.

Note that in all cases a 'pure' TS alternative occurs: each TS type is either produced internally or bought externally.

6.4. Establishment of the overall production plan

The overall approach assumes that the firm is directed by one single decision-maker, the central unit, that has complete information about the entire company. The central unit utilizes its knowledge on all sub-units in the firm to compute an overall solution, i.e. an optimal solution to the MIP problem as presented in table 6.1. This MIP problem formally represents the overall production planning problem the firm is faced with. In the present section we will describe in which way the central unit can establish a production plan according to the computed overall solution: the overall production plan.

The overall solution can immediately be translated in terms of production and sales levels, internally available TS, production techniques and so on. Hence the central unit could, in principle, establish the overall plan centrally and simply announce to each division the corresponding production and sales schedules, and the technology alternative to be applied. But a similar centralized approach clearly overrules the divisions. Therefore the following two-stage method seems more appropriate.

As a first step the central unit computes an overall solution in order to decide upon the following interrelated problems:
- How many of which TS-types must be produced internally?
- How should internally produced TS be allocated over the divisions?
- How should CR, capacities of which are constant, be allocated over the divisions?

Secondly, the central unit announces to each division its CR allocation a_n^{opt} and its internal-TS allocation b_n^{opt}. Here b_n^{opt} follows directly from the overall solution and $a_n^{opt} := A_n x_n^{opt}$ ($n=1,\ldots,N$).

Every division, in turn, determines its own production and sales plan, including the technology alternative to be applied and the amount of TS to be purchased externally. The whole set of divisional plans is firm-wide optimal if each division optimally uses its CR and internal-TS portions, i.e. if each division solves its problem

$$\text{Maximize} \quad -c_n x_n - dy_n + p_n z_n$$

$$\text{s.t.} \quad A_n x_n \leq a_n^{opt}$$

$$B_n x_n - y_n \leq b_n^{opt}$$

$$(I_n - D_n)x_n - z_n = 0$$

$$z_n \leq f_n$$

$$x_n, y_n, z_n \geq 0 \tag{6.3}$$

and then plans to produce, buy and sell according to the optimal values of x_n, y_n and z_n, respectively.

Now suppose that the optimum to MIP problem (6.1) is uniquely determined. Then the division will ultimately come up with $\hat{x}_n$, $\hat{y}_n$, $\hat{z}_n$ that coincide with this unique overall optimal solution. From section 6.2 we know that it is possible that, instead of a pure technology alternative, mixed techniques occur. Secondly, instead of the strict distinction between profitable product, to be sold maximally, and unprofitable products, not to be sold at all, there is also a 'transient' class of products which are sold but not maximally. As the divisions will determine solutions that are overall optimal, the just mentioned properties of overall solutions will indeed be observed at the local level.

6.5. Incorporation of cost allocation mechanisms

As outlined above, the establishment of the overall production plan develops in two stages. Firstly, the central unit decides upon the TS to be produced internally. Secondly, the divisions independently determine their production plans given certain amounts of CR and internal-TS as allocated by the central unit. Now we describe how a cost allocation mechanism can be incorporated.

At this point, a clarification concerning the word 'allocation' is in order. The announcement of CR and internal-TS portions to divisions are typical examples of an <u>allocation of input factors</u>. On the other hand, <u>allocation of costs</u>, as extensively discussed in chapter three, refers to a setting in which a number of cost objects (e.g. divisions, products) each bear an appropriate fraction of certain costs. Here we use the term 'allocation' in both senses.

6.5.1. <u>The allocation of internal-TS costs</u>

As part of the overall solution the central unit has found optimal make-or-buy decisions. Some TS-types are to be produced and supplied internally, the other TS-types are to be bought externally. In section 3.3.2 we argued that it is reasonable to allocate the costs of internally produced TS to users of that service. In brief, allocating costs of internal TS may stimulate prudent usage, while the TS producing departments will be required to operate efficiently and to satisfy the demands of the users. In this section it is supposed that the central unit has already determined the TS-types to be produced internally and also the amounts of internal TS are to be allocated to the divisions. Now the idea is to announce the portions of internal TS to each of the divisions together with a per-unit price for these internally supplied services. Below we describe the computation of this price.

Recall that as soon as two or more TS-types are produced internally these services may also deliver to each other. Thereby the computation of the correct price to be charged to the users is complicated. However, in these circumstances the reciprocal allocation method (see section 3.3.2) can be fruitfully applied. Being originally introduced and clarified for a situation in which all TS-types are produced internally, the method is easily adapted to the present circumstances, with only a subset of TS-types internally produced and supplied.

We now give the formulas that summarize the (modified) reciprocal allocation method. Suppose we have at hand x_0^{opt}, y_0^{opt} and δ^{opt} (as elements of an overall solution). From Theorem 6.2 we know that $x_0^{opt}(m) > 0$ and $y_0^{opt}(m) > 0$ do not occur simultaneously, $m=1,\ldots,M$. Here M denotes the number of TS-types. For notational convenience we assume that for each m $x_0^{opt}(m) + y_0^{opt}(m) > 0$. The diagonal matrix $\text{diag}[x_0^{opt};y_0^{opt}]$ and its inverse $\text{diag}^{-1}[x_0^{opt}; y_0^{opt}]$ are defined as follows:

$$\text{diag}[x_0^{opt};y_0^{opt}]_{mm} := x_0^{opt}(m) + y_0^{opt}(m), \qquad m=1,\ldots,M \qquad (6.4)$$

$$\text{diag}^{-1}[x_0^{opt};y_0^{opt}]_{mm} := (x_0^{opt}(m) + y_0^{opt}(m))^{-1}, \quad m=1,\dots,M \tag{6.5}$$

Let C^{opt} and c^{opt} be the (row) vectors of fixed costs and per-unit direct costs, i.e. $(m=1,\dots,M)$

$$C^{opt}(m) := C(m)\ \delta^{opt}(m),$$
$$c^{opt}(m) := c(m)\ \delta^{opt}(m) + d(m)(1-\delta^{opt}(m)) \tag{6.6}$$

The input-output matrix of optimal TS alternative δ^{opt} is denoted by D_0^{opt}; its columns are given by

$$(D_0^{opt})_{*m} := (D_0)_{*m}\ \delta^{opt}(m), \quad m=1,\dots,M. \tag{6.7}$$

Now we can give the formula for the per-unit redistributed costs, namely

$$g := (c^{opt} + C^{opt}\text{diag}^{-1}[x_0^{opt};y_0^{opt}])(I-D_0^{opt})^{-1} \tag{6.8}$$

The components of g are the prices for each TS type. If TS_m is bought externally, it will turn out that $g(m) = d(m)$. If TS_m is produced internally, $g(m)$ is the internal price for this service to be charged to all users. Now suppose division n obtains an amount $b_n^{opt}(m)$ of internal TS_m. By charging price $g(m)$, the central unit allocates a cost equal to $g(m)$ times $b_n^{opt}(m)$ to division n.

In this way all redistributed costs of TS_m are allocated with consumption of TS_m as the allocation basis.

6.5.2. <u>Common cost allocation</u>

The second class of costs to be allocated are the costs of the sector general services (GS). The GS sector performs activities from which the firm as a whole benefits. The incurred costs are therefore called 'common costs'. Similar to internally produced TS, the output of the GS sector is not delivered to the outside market, so that the common costs have to be allocated. However, the common costs are entirely fixed and, in the short run, it is impossible to measure each subunit's benefit from GS activities. Hence, lacking any natural allocation basis, any mechanism for common cost allocation will suffer from a certain degree of arbitrariness. As a minimum requirement, the common costs must be allocated without provoking suboptimal decisions. In this book, focusing on planning in a general divisionalized enterprise, this requirement implies that some allocation mechanism for common costs must not distort the overall production plan.

The planning problem we are dealing with is formally represented by a MIP problem. But if one fixes the integer variables at their optimal value a continuous LP problem is obtained. As discussed in section 3.3.3, Kaplan and Thompson (1971) addressed the problem of allocating a fixed cost in the context of an LP model of the firm. In this section we will demonstrate how that cost allocation method can be adapted to our MIP formulation of the planning problem.

Recall that two pieces of information were required for applying the LP based cost allocation method as introduced in section 3.3.3. Firstly, one has to know the shadow price for (a subset of) the resources needed in the production process. Secondly, the available amounts of these resources must be known and then multiplied by the shadow price vector. This multiplication yields the valuation of the considered resources and is required to be larger than the costs to be allocated.

Returning to our planning problem, suppose that the central unit has announced to each division its CR allocation a_n^{opt} and internal-TS allocation b_n^{opt}. In section 6.3 we explained that the divisions can determine production plans which are firm-wide optimal by solving problems (6.2), $n=1,\ldots,N$. In addition the central unit will now ask each division to report its per-unit valuation of allocated CR. Formally, an optimal dual variable $\hat{\pi}_n^{opt}$ associated with constraint $A_n x_n \leq a_n^{opt}$ is required. All divisional responses together yield a valuation $V(a) :=$ $\sum_{n=1}^{N} \hat{\pi}_n^{opt} a_n^{opt}$ of the total CR capacity.

Now let the common costs be equal to H and suppose they are smaller than the total valuation of CR, i.e. $H < V(a)$. Then the fraction h defined as $h := H/V(a)$ is smaller than 1. Secondly, let p_n^{opt} be the optimal solution value to (6.3), i.e. p_n^{opt} is the contribution to the profit by division n. If each division solves the problem

$$\text{Maximize} \ -(c_n + h\pi_n^{opt}A_n)x_n - dy_n + p_nz_n$$

$$\text{s.t.} \qquad A_nx_n \qquad\qquad \leqslant a_n^{opt}$$

$$B_nx_n - y_n \qquad\quad \leqslant b_n^{opt}$$

$$(I_n - D_n)x_n \qquad - z_n = 0$$

$$z_n \leqslant f_n$$

$$x_n, y_n, z_n \geqslant 0 \tag{6.9}$$

then the originally optimal $\hat{x}_n$, $\hat{y}_n$, $\hat{z}_n$ (i.e. optimal to (6.3)) are again optimal and the optimal solution value is $P_n^{opt} - h\hat{\pi}_n^{opt}a_n^{opt}$. Hence the overall production plan is maintained and the divisions together realize a contribution to profit equal to $\sum_{n=1}^{N}(P_n^{opt} - h\hat{\pi}_n^{opt}a_n) = \sum_{n=1}^{N}P_n^{opt} - H$. But this means that the sum of the original profit contributions is maintained while a cost equal to H is allocated.

6.6. Summary

The planning problem related to our general model of the firm was analysed from an overall point of view. Hence organizational aspects were neglected and the central unit was assumed to have full information. In these circumstances the central unit can immediately compute an overall solution. However, the divisions participated actively in the elaboration of the overall production plan, i.e. a production plan according to the overall solution as computed by the central unit.

Finally, we saw that it is possible to allocate common costs and internal-TS costs without distortion of the overall production plan. In particular, certain properties of the overall solution (e.g. simultaneous use of more than one technique for a specific market product) are maintained.

CHAPTER SEVEN

MULTILEVEL ANALYSIS OF THE MODEL OF THE FIRM

7.1. Introduction

This chapter embodies our contribution to the theory on multilevel decisions in a general, decentralized enterprise. We will investigate the model of the firm within the conceptual framework for multilevel planning as introduced in chapter four. So the model will be studied with explicit attention for organizational features, in particular the issue of localized information.

We will start with a review of multilevel features as included in our model of the firm (section 7.2). Then we will propose a planning procedure in which the central unit and the divisions exchange information in their search for techniques and make-or-buy decisions that are desired for the company as a whole (section 7.3). Costs will be allocated carefully. As cost allocations should not distort the firm-wide optimum, their incorporation in the planning process should, at least, not damage the information exchange in the firm (section 7.4).

In earlier work (Meijboom (1986)), we proposed a similar planning procedure including cost allocations. The present chapter provides more insight into the divisional contribution to the planning process. Secondly, we propose an improved method for common cost allocation.

7.2. The multilevel approach for decentralized firms

Here we briefly review the general model of the firm, in particular the proposed organizational structure. First of all, we repeat the main arguments why a multilevel scope cannot be left out from the present economic context.

In every real-world company of a reasonable size a certain degree of decentralization has taken place. A number of product divisions and service departments exist and the information to make decisions is dispersed among these subunits. Thus many existing firms consist of more or less independently acting subunits to be coordinated by a central unit at a higher organizational level. The central unit gathers information from subunits before the final plan can be established and allocates costs during this planning process.

With this view of the reality of decentralized companies, we developed a model of the firm along the following lines. See also figure 7.1.

The divisions in the firm produce the commodities that can be sold on the external market. For each of these market products more than one technique may be available. The divisions operate relatively independently of each other and are viewed as profit centres. They are connected through the joint use of internally produced technical services (TS). Secondly, the divisions share a number of facilities and materials referred to as common resources (CR).

Apart from production supported by TS the firm has a sector general services (GS). The GS departments produce common goods from which the firm as a whole benefits. These activities result in common costs.

The central unit of the firm is responsible for the total net profit, i.e. the sum of divisional profits minus internal-TS costs and common costs. Furthermore, the output of TS and GS departments is not sold outside the firm, so the central unit must allocate the internal-TS costs and the common costs.

As a natural consequence of specialization and localization of information, we suppose the following two-level organizational structure. At the lower level, there are the divisions. Each of them possesses specific knowledge with respect to its techniques, market restrictions etc., not known to other subunits. At the top level, there is the central unit, which decides whether to make or to buy technical services, which coordinates the distribution of CR and internal TS, and allocates costs, namely internal-TS costs and common costs. The crucial difficulty for the central unit is its incomplete information about the divisions.

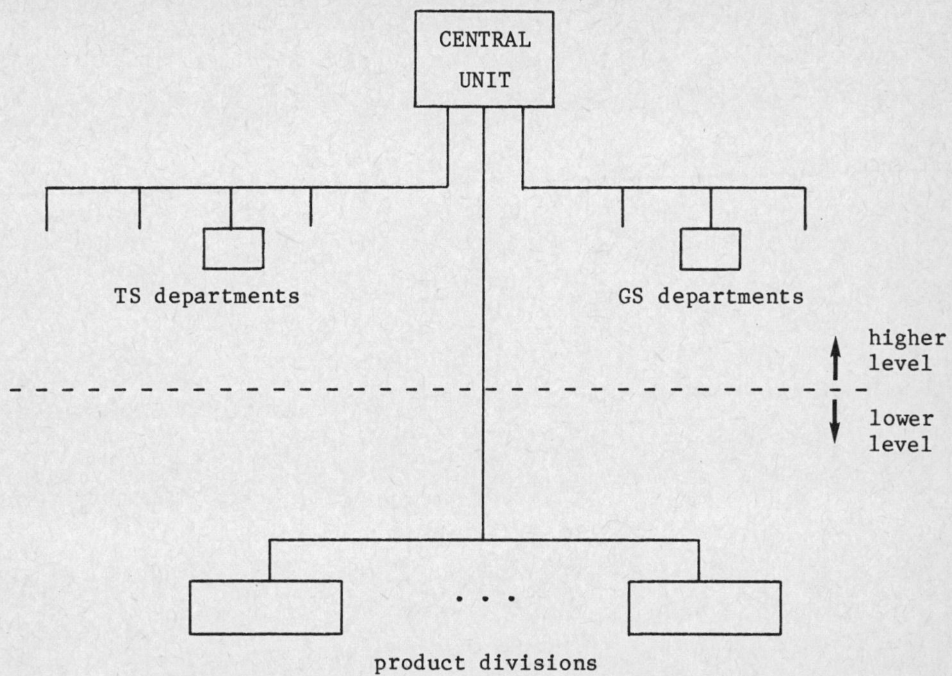

<u>Figure 7.1</u>: Organizational structure

The overall planning problem the firm is faced with consists of two parts, namely:

1. The problem of determining firm-wide optimal production techniques and make-or-buy decisions without overconsumption of the common resources. This problem is formally represented by MIP problem (3.6) in table 3.1.

2. The problem of allocating common costs and the costs of producing TS internally.

Because of its incomplete information about the divisions, the central unit cannot formulate and solve a fully specified version of the MIP problem. Firstly the central unit has to resolve its problem of lack of information with respect to the divisions in the firm. To this end it initiates a decomposition-based planning procedure. Such a procedure embodies a sequence of planning sessions during which the central unit and the divisions exchange information. The major part of the planning

Maximize	$-c_1x_1 - dy_1 + p_1z_1$	$-c_2x_2 - dy_2 + p_2z_2$	$\cdots$	$-c_Nx_N - dy_N + p_Nz_N$		$-c_0x_0 - dy_0 - C\delta$		
s.t.	A_1x_1				$-a_1$		≤ 0	
	$B_1x_1 - y_1$				$-b_1$		≤ 0	division 1
	$(I_1 - D_1)x_1 - z_1$						$= 0$	
	z_1						$\leq f_1$	
		A_2x_2			$-a_2$		≤ 0	
		$B_2x_2 - y_2$			$-b_2$		≤ 0	division 2
		$(I_2 - D_2)x_2 - z_2$					$= 0$	
		z_2					$\leq f_2$	
		$\vdots$					$\vdots$	
				A_Nx_N	$-a_N$		≤ 0	
				$B_Nx_N - y_N$	$-b_N$		≤ 0	division N
				$(I_N - D_N)x_N - z_N$			$= 0$	
				z_N			$\leq f_N$	
					$a_1 + a_2 \cdots + a_N$		$= a$	CR allocation
					$b_1 + b_2 \cdots + b_N - b_0$		$= 0$	
					b_0		$-W\delta \leq 0$	TS allocation
						$b_0 - (I - D_0)x_0 - y_0$	$= 0$	
						x_0	$-W\delta \leq 0$	TS production

all x_n, y_n, z_n, a_n, $b_n \geq 0$

δ : 0–1 vector

W : large positive constant

Table 7.2: Problem (7.1): reformulated overall planning problem.

phase in the decision-making process is thus devoted to the planning sessions of this procedure. At the end of the planning phase the central unit has collected sufficient information to establish a final plan and to allocate costs.

7.3. <u>Proposal for a two-level planning procedure</u>

The planning procedure in which the central unit gathers the necessary information to solve the planning problem will now be presented. We do not consider cost allocation mechanisms yet; this issue is treated in the next section.

As a start we slightly modify the MIP problem according to table 7.2. This reformulated equivalent problem formulation shows that the central unit is dealing with the following three interrelated problems:
- How much of which TS-types must be produced internally?
- How should the internally produced TS be allocated over the divisions?
- How should the CR, the capacities of which are constant, be allocated over the divisions?

The decision variables associated to these problems are $\{x_0, y_0, b_0, \delta\}$, $\{b_1, \ldots, b_N\}$ and $\{a_1, \ldots, a_N\}$ respectively. Throughout this chapter we assume that problem (7.1) has an optimal solution with finite solution value.

The planning procedure as described in section 4.4 can also be applied if a subset of the variables is not continuous (e.g. integer variables) provided they occur in the central unit's part of the decomposed problem. In the present situation there are 0-1 variables (vector δ) due to occurrence of make-or-buy decisions including fixed cost components. Therefore we propose a resource-directive procedure in which (tentative) decisions concerning δ, i.e. concerning TS alternatives, are not 'delegated' to the divisions. In each planning session the central unit confronts the divisions with tentative amounts of CR and internally available TS. The divisions, in turn, respond with per-unit valuations for the allocated resources and services. In section 7.3.2 we will investigate in more detail how each intermediate allocation of CR and TS affects the tentative divisional activity plans. Subsequently, we will analyse the information contents of the data as exchanged between top level and lower level (section 7.3.3). We start with an introductory description of the proposed planning procedure.

7.3.1. Outline of the planning procedure

Based on the current divisional information as available at the top level, tentative amounts of CR and internal TS, $\bar{a}_n^k$ and $\bar{b}_n^k$ respectively, are computed. At the same time, estimates $\bar{P}_n^k$ for the divisional profits given $\bar{a}_n^k$ and $\bar{b}_n^k$ are determined. Here k denotes the current planning session. Subsequently, each division is asked to compute its profit $\hat{P}_n^k$ given $\bar{a}_n^k$ and $\bar{b}_n^k$. Formally, each division solves

$$
\begin{aligned}
\text{Maximize} \quad & - c_n x_n - dy_n + p_n z_n \\
\text{s.t.} \quad A_n x_n \quad & \leqslant \bar{a}_n^k \\
B_n x_n - y_n \quad & \leqslant \bar{b}_n^k \\
(I_n - D_n)x_n \quad - \quad z_n & = 0 \\
z_n & \leqslant f_n \\
x_n, y_n, z_n & \geqslant 0
\end{aligned}
\tag{7.2}
$$

and $\hat{P}_n^k$ is the optimal solution value of problem (7.2).

The estimates $\bar{P}_n^k$ as computed by the central unit are optimistic: the actual divisional profits $\hat{P}_n^k$ will not exceed these estimates: $\hat{P}_n^k \leqslant \bar{P}_n^k$ for all n. Optimality of the current $\bar{P}_n^k$, $\bar{a}_n^k$, $\bar{b}_n^k$ is now tested by checking whether $\bar{P}_n^k \leqslant \hat{P}_n^k$ for all n. If this is so, the latest allocations $\bar{a}_n^k$, $\bar{b}_n^k$ of CR and internal TS and the associated profit estimates $\bar{P}_n^k$ are optimal for the firm as a whole and the procedure is terminated. Otherwise, if at least one estimate of divisional profit exceeds the actual profit of that division, the central unit will ask the division's per-unit valuations of $\bar{a}_n^k$ and $\bar{b}_n^k$. Formally, the optimal dual variables $\hat{\pi}_n^k$ and $\hat{\rho}_n^k$ associated with the divisional CR constraints $A_n x_n \leqslant \bar{a}_n^k$ and TS constraints $B_n x_n - y_n \leqslant \bar{b}_n^k$ respectively are required. The per-unit valuations contain sufficient information for the central unit to derive improved profit estimates in the next planning session. The procedure is terminated as soon as the central unit has gathered sufficient information to determine company-wide optimal allocations of CR and internal TS. This will occur after a finite number of planning sessions.

The outline of the planning procedure presented above is very brief and superficial. See also figure 7.3. In the remainder of this chapter the gaps will be filled. We will work out several aspects of the procedure and add cost allocation mechanisms, thus building up the complete description of the planning process in our two-level divisionalized company. We continue with a further analysis of the divisional contribution to the planning procedure.

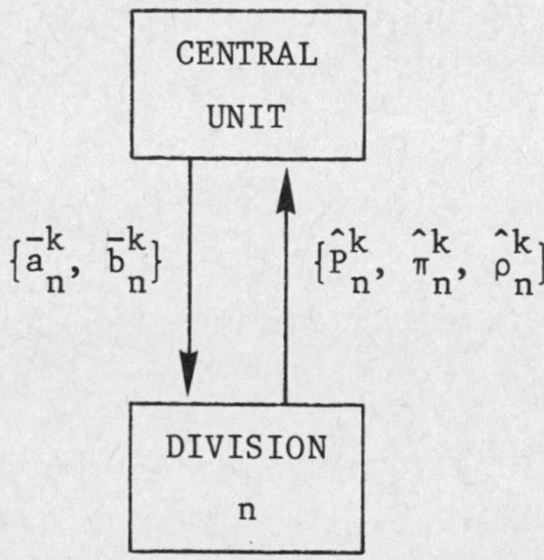

Figure 7.3: Information exchange in k-th planning session.

7.3.2. Intermediate divisional activity plans

In this section the divisional plans and calculations as occurring during the planning sessions will be analysed. Recall that each division is repeatedly asked to solve problem (7.2). For the planning procedure to succeed, it is sufficient if each division reports its profit and per-unit valuation of each CR type and TS type to the central unit. However, from a model-building point of view, a few more questions should be answered. For instance, how many techniques are involved in the n-th division if it optimally utilizes the allocated resources and services? The purpose of this section is to investigate the primal solution to problem (7.2) in more detail. As the related decision variables x_n, y_n, z_n represent the n-th division's planned production, purchase and sales, it is reasonable to call the primal solution to (7.2) the <u>divisional activity plan</u>.

In general, the tentative allocations of CR and internal TS will lead to divisional activity plans in which for some product types more than one technique is involved. Or, certain product types occur that are supplied to the outside market, but below the outside demand level. To understand this, consider the hypothetical situation in which a division can ignore the CR and TS constraints, for instance because the division at hand does not require any CR or TS. Then the division's remaining problem is to find a technology alternative by which it can maximize its individual profit. From chapter two, in particular from the analysis related to problems (2.2) and (2.3), we know that some profit maximizing production schedule always exists that applies not more than one technique per product. Secondly, the profitable products are sold maximally, the unprofitable products are not sold at all.

However, the CR constraints are not redundant. This means: the division may well be allocated CR portions that set a limit to the production intensities and thus to the sales levels, given the original profit maximizing (and pure) technology alternative as introduced in the preceding paragraph. In order to cope with the CR shortage, the division could lower the production and sales levels of certain product types. An alternative would be to mix the original pure technology alternative with another technology alternative that uses less CR than the original one. Then at least one product applies more than one technique.

Of course, the allocation of internal TS to divisions in limited amounts could similarly yield 'mixed techniques' and/or 'decreased sales levels'. But a third way exists for TS to overcome shortages, namely additional external purchase of services. From an overall point of view, i.e. considering the firm as a whole, we saw that each TS-type is either produced internally or bought externally (cf. chapter six, section 6.3). However, during the planning procedure the tentative allocation of internal TS could tempt that division to plan additional external purchase of these services.

Altogether, when faced with some intermediate allocation of CR and internal TS, a division has several options to resolve eventual shortages of these input factors, briefly speaking 'mixed techniques', 'decreased sales levels' and 'external TS purchase'. We now present a theorem concerning the number of applied techniques, the number of product types with decreased sales levels and the number of TS-types that are internally supplied to some division and planned to be additionally bought from outside the firm by that division.

As a matter of fact, the theorem below states a property of optimal basic solutions to a modified but equivalent version of problem (7.2).

It is assumed that we are considering a division that faces a positive outside demand for each of its product types, i.e. $f_n > 0$. It requires all CR-types and is therefore allocated tentative CR portions each of which is positive. Furthermore, from the TS constraints $B_n x_n - y_n \leq \bar{b}_n^k$ we omit the rows the right-hand side of which (i.e. $\bar{b}_n^k(m)$ for some m) are equal to zero. The remaining constraints, denoted by $\tilde{B}_n x_n - \tilde{y}_n \leq \tilde{b}_n^k$, are concerned with TS-types that are indeed supplied to the division: $\tilde{b}_n^k > 0$. If additional amounts of these TS-types are still (planned to be) bought externally, the associated costs are $\tilde{\tilde{d}}\tilde{y}_n$. The TS-types that were not internally supplied at all have to be bought entirely from outside the firm. The associated costs are assumed to be accounted for in the direct costs of production and we write $\tilde{c}_n x_n$ instead of $c_n x_n$.

The modified formulation of the divisional planning problem is thus:

$$
\begin{aligned}
\text{Maximize} \quad & - \tilde{c}_n x_n - \tilde{\tilde{d}}\tilde{y}_n + p_n z_n \\
\text{s.t.} \quad & A_n x_n && \leq \bar{a}_n^k \\
& \tilde{B}_n x_n - \tilde{y}_n && \leq \tilde{b}_n^k \\
& (I_n - D_n)x_n - z_n && = 0 \\
& z_n && \leq f_n \\
& x_n, y_n, z_n \geq 0
\end{aligned}
\tag{7.3}
$$

and $\bar{a}_n^k > 0$, $\tilde{b}_n^k > 0$, $f_n > 0$. Recall that Φ_n denotes the number of product types of division n and that there are L different CR-types. We have:

Theorem 7.1

Consider an optimal basic solution to problem (7.3) with $\bar{a}_n^k > 0$, $\tilde{b}_n^k > 0$, $f_n > 0$. For this solution:

1. we assume that for each product at least one technique is applied;
2. we define μ_n^k, β_n^k, SA_n^k, SB_n^k, σ_n^k and θ_n^k as follows:

μ_n^k := the number of applied techniques, so $\mu_n^k \geq \Phi_n$;

β_n^k := the number of product types that are sold but below the outside demand level, so $0 \leqslant \beta_n^k \leqslant \Phi_n$;

SA_n^k := the number of CR-types that are not fully used up, so $0 \leqslant SA_n^k \leqslant L$;

M_n^k := the dimension of $\tilde{b}_n^k$, i.e. the number of TS-types that are internally supplied to division n;

SB_n^k := the number of TS-types that are internally supplied but not fully used up, so $0 \leqslant SB_n^k \leqslant M_n^k$;

σ_n^k := the number of TS-types that are internally supplied and also bought from outside the firm, so $0 \leqslant \sigma_n^k \leqslant M_n^k$;

θ_n^k := the number of basic zeros.

Now it holds that:

$$\sigma_n^k + SB_n^k \leqslant M_n^k, \tag{7.4-a}$$

$$(\mu_n^k - \Phi_n) + \beta_n^k + \sigma_n^k = (L - SA_n^k) + (M_n^k - SB_n^k) - \theta_n^k \tag{7.4-b}$$

Proof: See Appendix F.

Similar to Theorem 6.2, this result does not give an economic explanation for mixing, decreased sales levels or external TS purchase. It is a statement of necessary conditions concerning divisional activity plans as occurring during the planning procedure. If we assume, in addition, non-degeneracy of the considered basic optimal solution (i.e. $\theta_n^k = 0$), we see that the more CR-types and internal-TS types are fully used up, the larger the number $L - SA_n^k + M_n^k - SB_n^k$, so the more mixing, decreased sales levels and/or additional external TS purchase must be noticed. A further comparison of Theorems 6.2 and 7.1 yields the following interesting difference: at intermediate instances in the planning process, additional external purchase of some internally supplied TS-type may well occur. Furthermore, the sum of the right-hand sides of (7.4-b) over all divisions counts the total amount of mixing, decreased sales levels and external TS purchase and can be much larger than in the optimal situation.

7.3.3. The information contents of exchanged data

In the previous section we focused on the details of intermediate divisional activity plans in response on tentative allocations of CR and internal TS. However, for the planning procedure to succeed, typically aggregated, so less detailed data can be submitted to the central unit. In the present section we further analyse the information contents of data as exchanged in the planning procedure. The analysis is centred around the following two questions:

- What concrete information can the central unit derive from the data collected up to 'now', i.e. at some intermediate instance within the planning phase?
- In which respect does the central unit enlarge its knowledge on the divisions in subsequent planning steps?

As noted before, the central unit has incomplete information with respect to the divisions. Hence it cannot solve the overall planning problem independently. Instead the divisions are asked to solve their part of the planning problem a number of times, given various, fixed CR and TS portions a_n^{-k} and b_n^{-k} respectively. In this way the central unit gathers information concerning each division's profit as a function of allocated CR and TS. These profit functions will be denoted by $P_n(a_n,b_n)$ with a_n,b_n as usual $(n=1,\ldots,N)$. Below we introduce a reformulated version of the overall planning problem in terms of $P_n(a_n,b_n)$ $(n=1,\ldots,N)$. Then we will clarify the information gathering process as occurring during the planning procedure.

Define the TS-production domain V by

$$V := \{(x_0,y_0,b_0,\delta) \mid (I - D_0)x_0 + y_0 - b_0 = 0; \ x_0 - W\delta \leqslant 0;$$
$$b_0 - W\delta \leqslant 0; \ x_0, \ y_0, \ b_0 \geqslant 0; \ \delta \ \text{0-1 vector}\} \quad (7.5)$$

and the divisional profit functions $P_n(a_n,b_n)$ $(n=1,\ldots,N)$ by

$$P_n(a_n,b_n) := \text{Max } \{-c_n x_n - dy_n + p_n z_n \mid A_n x_n \leqslant a_n; \ B_n x_n - y_n \leqslant b_n;$$

$$(I_n - D_n)x_n - z_n = 0; \ z_n \leqslant f_n; \ x_n, \ y_n, \ z_n \geqslant 0\} \quad (7.6)$$

The overall planning problem can be written as:

$$\text{Maximize } (- c_0 x_0 - dy_0 - C\delta + \sum_{n=1}^{N} P_n(a_n,b_n))$$

$$\text{s.t.} \quad (x_0,y_0,b_0,\delta) \in V, \ \sum_{n=1}^{N} b_n - b_0 = 0, \ \sum_{n=1}^{N} a_n = a,$$

$$\text{all } a_n, \ b_n \geqslant 0 \quad (7.7)$$

The terms $c_0 x_0 + dy_0 + C\delta$ are the costs of internally supplied TS. Formulation (7.7) explicitly represents the problem of the central unit of determining allocations a_n, b_n $(n=1,\ldots,N)$ such that the sum of the divisional profits minus the internal-TS costs is maximal.

Immediate solution of this problem would be possible if the divisional profits were known by the central unit for all possible CR and TS allocations. Of course, this requirement cannot be met. In the assumed organizational conditions the central unit has only limited insight into the production and sales opportunities of each division. Hence the central unit cannot fully know profit functions $P_n(a_n,b_n)$ $(n=1,\ldots,N)$.

The purpose of the planning procedure is to generate information on the basis of which the functions $P_n(a_n,b_n)$ can be approximated. In each separate planning session divisions report their maximal profit $\hat{P}_n^k$ and per-unit valuations $\hat{\pi}_n^k$, $\hat{\rho}_n^k$ of the (tentatively) allocated CR and internal TS. These data can be used to derive a linear function that approximates $P_n(a_n,b_n)$ in the following way:

$$P_n(a_n,b_n) \leqslant \hat{P}_n^k + \hat{\pi}_n^k (a_n - \bar{a}_n^k) + \hat{\rho}_n^k (b_n - \bar{b}_n^k), \quad a_n, \ b_n \geqslant 0 \quad (7.8)$$

At an intermediate instance in the planning procedure, i.e. after a number of planning sessions, the central unit has generated some linear approximations of type (7.8) for each division's real (but unknown) profit function $P_n(a_n,b_n)$. Hence, combining the data as generated up to this point in the planning process, the central unit can derive piecewise-linear approximations of each of the divisional profit functions $P_n(a_n, b_n)$.

The central unit computes the CR and internal TS allocations of the next planning session by solving (7.7) with each $P_n(a_n, b_n)$ replaced by its approximating function. As these piecewise-linear approximations majorize the real profit functions (recall inequality (7.8)), the central unit obtains an upper bound, i.e. an optimistic 'estimate' of the total profit. Therefore we say that the partial information concerning the divisional profit functions is used in an optimistic way.

Subsequent planning sessions yield additional divisional information and help to improve the piecewise-linear approximating functions. For the more inequalities of the form (7.8) are known to the central unit, the better it is able to 'estimate' the divisional profit functions. Note that the data as reported to the central unit in each separate planning session have a rather limited information contents. It is the succession of planning sessions, however, that enables the central unit to 'build up' improving approximations of divisional profit functions.

In section 7.3.2 we investigated the intermediate divisional activity plans in a rather detailed way, particularly the occurrence of mixing, decreased sales levels and additional external TS purchase (cf. Theorem 7.1). None of these three options can be foreseen separately; they are interrelated and follow from the (primal) solution of divisional problem (7.2). In the planning procedure, however, the central unit is not interested in the complete specifications of planned activities given CR and TS allocations as calculated in each division. The central unit is satisfied with information of an essentially less detailed, more aggregated nature namely divisional profits and per-unit valuations of allocated resources and services. What can we say about the meaning of these valuations?

In section 7.3.2 we argued that in some planning session a shortage of CR and/or TS is likely to occur in divisions. Hence the per-unit valuation or shadow price of the corresponding CR or TS constraints in problem (7.2) seems to be interpretable in terms of these shortages. However, suppose that a shortage of some CR-type is resolved by mixing of techniques. In turn, the latter 'reaction' may cause a shortage of some TS-type to be resolved by additional external purchase. More generally, scarcity of CR and TS are interrelated and these mutual dependencies will ultimately be accounted for in the per-unit valuations of allocated CR and TS.

7.3.4. Numerical example

The presentation of the planning procedure is of a rather formal and general nature. Just like in chapter six, matters will be further clarified by means of the numerical example introduced there.

Recall that in this example we consider a firm with two divisions. The central unit is faced with make-or-buy decisions for three TS-types and must allocate two types of CR. Below we describe a simulation of the planning procedure as outlined earlier. The CR-capacity vector $a = (a(1), a(2))$ is taken equal to $(80, 60)$, so the total profit should turn out to be 33882.13 at the end of the procedure (cf. section 6.3, table 6.3).

Initially $(k=1)$ the central unit proposes not to produce and supply TS internally, i.e. $\delta^k = (0,0,0)$ (see table 7.4) and all $b_n^1(\cdot) = 0$ (see table 7.4), and to allocate to each division half of the total CR capacity, i.e. $a_1^1(1) = a_2^1(1) = 40$ and $a_1^1(2) = a_2^1(2) = 30$ (see table 7.4). Having no information at all, the initial estimates by the central unit of divisional profits are both ∞, while no TS costs are incurred (see table 7.4). Formally, this follows from the initial 'relaxed master problem' given by

$$\text{Maximize} - c_0 x_0 - dy_0 - C\delta + P_1 + P_2$$
$$\text{s.t.} \quad (x_0, y_0, b_0, \delta) \in V, \; b_1 + b_2 - b_0 = 0, \; a_1 + a_2 = a,$$
$$a_1, b_1, a_2, b_2 \geqslant 0 \tag{7.9}$$

an optimal solution of which is $\bar{P}_1, \bar{P}_2 = \infty$; $\bar{x}_0, \bar{y}_0, \bar{\delta}, \bar{b}_0, \bar{b}_1, \bar{b}_2 = 0$; $a_1 = a_2 = 0.5a$.

Subsequently, the divisions compute their profits $\hat{P}_n^1$, $n=1,2$, and their per-unit valuations $\hat{\pi}_n(\cdot)$, $\hat{\rho}_n(\cdot)$, $n=1,2$, of allocated CR and TS, and report them to the central unit. See table 7.4. Note for instance that the per-unit valuation of TS_1, by division 1, equals market price $d(1)$

105

(= 165). Indeed, one extra unit of internal TS_1 would reduce the external purchase costs of this service with 165 units of money.

As $\hat{P}_1^1 < \bar{P}_1^1$ and $\hat{P}_2^1 < \bar{P}_2^1$ the central unit adds constraints of form (7.8) to problem (7.9), viz.

$$P_1 - 143.49\, a_1(2) - 165\, b_1(1) - 65\, b_1(3) \leqslant 7333.33, \qquad (7.10\text{-a})$$

$$P_2 - 195\, b_2(2) - 65\, b_2(3) \leqslant 18721.23 \qquad (7.10\text{-b})$$

and resolves modified problem (7.9): a new planning session starts.

The central unit ultimately finds the total profit for the firm as a whole in the 10th planning session, i.e. $k = 10$. The results of this sequence of 10 planning sessions are listed in table 7.4.

In table 7.4 we have listed the tentative make-or-buy decisions, the associated costs, the profit estimates for division 1 and 2 and the estimate of the total profit $\bar{P}_1^{-k} + \bar{P}_2^{-k} - c_0 x_0^{-k} - d y_0^{-k} - C\delta^{-k}$. It is worthwile to note that the latter estimates, $k = 1,2,\ldots$ form a decreasing sequence of upper bounds for the correct (but unknown) total profit. On the other hand, the estimates of the divisional profit $\bar{P}_1^{-k}$ $(k=1,2\ldots)$ and $\bar{P}_2^{-k}$ $(k=1,2,\ldots)$ are not monotonic. See figure 7.5.

The remainder of table 7.4 is concerned with the divisions. Given the CR and internal-TS allocations $(\bar{a}_n^{-k}(\cdot),\ \bar{b}_n^{-k}(\cdot),\ n=1,2)$, the divisional responses $(\bar{\pi}_n(\cdot),\ \hat{\rho}_n(\cdot),\ \hat{P}_n^k,\ n=1,2)$ are listed. The final column $\hat{\eta}_n^k f_n$ is merely added for explanatory purposes. Each $\hat{\eta}_n^k f_n$ is actually computed by the central unit to be used as right-hand sides in constraints such as (7.10) $(\hat{\eta}_n^k f_n = \hat{P}_n^k - \hat{\pi}_n^k \bar{a}_n^{-k} - \hat{\rho}_n^k \bar{b}_n^{-k})$. Note that before reaching optimality we have $\bar{P}_n^{-k} > \hat{P}_n^k$ for at least one n. In figure 7.5 this is further illustrated.

To conclude the numerical illustration, a few considerations are in order with respect to (intermediate) divisional activity plans. As an example we have listed the divisional solutions in the fourth planning session. See table 7.6. Division 1 has lowered the sales level of product $X_{1,1}$, viz. $z_1(1) = 14.60 < 18$, while one CR-type is not fully used up and no external TS is additionally bought. Division 2 uses two techniques for product $X_{2,1}$ and has lowered the sales level of this

Table 7.4 Profit and shadow prices as reported by the divisions given the CR and internal TS allocations in the subsequent planning sessions.

step k	TS alternative $\bar{\delta}^k$			TS costs $c_0\bar{x}_0^k+d\bar{y}_0^k+C\bar{\delta}^k$	estimate of:		total profit
					profit contribution of division 1 and 2 $\bar{P}_1^k$	$\bar{P}_2^k$	
1	0	0	0	0	∞	∞	∞
2	0	1	1	28951.10	28400.87	53821.23	53271.00
3	0	1	1	28951.10	15178.48	66279.52	52506.90
4	0	1	1	28951.10	15178.48	63144.67	49372.05
5	1	1	1	43800.00	40300.50	51217.10	47717.59
6	1	1	0	40474.59	45904.02	37590.00	43019.43
7	1	1	1	35894.46	33616.66	37590.00	35312.20
8	0	1	1	17937.45	15178.48	37590.00	34831.03
9	0	1	1	18217.75	14758.72	37590.00	34130.97
10	0	1	1	17900.10	14742.64	37040.00	33882.13

Tentative TS alternatives and profit estimates as computed by the central unit in the subsequent planning sessions.

DIVISION 1:

step k	common resources				internal-TS supply				profit given CR/TS portions $\hat{P}_1^k$	valuation market restriction $\hat{\eta}_1^k f_1$
	allocated CR_1 $\bar{a}_1^k(1)$	shadow price $\hat{\pi}_1^k(1)$	allocated CR_2 $\bar{a}_1^k(2)$	shadow price $\hat{\pi}_1^k(2)$	allocated TS_1 $\bar{b}_1^k(1)$	shadow price $\hat{\rho}_1^k(1)$	allocated TS_3 $\bar{b}_1^k(s)$	shadow price $\hat{\rho}_1^k(3)$		
1	40.00	0	30.00	143.49	0	165	0	65	11637.95	7333.33
2	80.00	0	60.00	0	0	165	191.67	0	15178.48	15178.48
3	51.56	0	54.67	0	0	165	0	65	12904.02	12904.02
4	51.56	0	32.83	202.07	0	165	48.23	0	13966.79	7333.33
5	0	1604.67	35.23	0	156.67	0	31.75	0	0	0
6	31.22	388.63	38.82	22.56	200.00	0	0	65	20343.67	7333.33
7	63.20	0	21.23	469.78	133.30	0	19.13	0	17305.23	7333.33
8	11.72	212.17	45.00	0	0	165	35.00	0	9820.22	7333.33
9	35.00	191.98	36.75	10.09	0	165	33.12	0	14423.09	7333.33
10	36.67	191.98	36.67	10.09	0	165	33.05	0	14742.64	7333.33

DIVISION 2:

step k	common resources				internal-TS supply				profit given CR/TS portions $\hat{P}_2^k$	valuation market restrictions $\hat{\eta}_2^k f_k$
	allocated CR_1 $\bar{a}_2^k(1)$	shadow price $\hat{\pi}_2^k(1)$	allocated CR_2 $\bar{a}_2^k(2)$	shadow price $\hat{\pi}_2^k(2)$	allocated TS_1 $\bar{b}_2^k(2)$	shadow price $\hat{\rho}_2^k(2)$	allocated TS_3 $\bar{b}_2^k(3)$	shadow price $\hat{\rho}_2^k(3)$		
1	40.00	0	30.00	0	0	195	0	65	18721.23	18721.23
2	0	1892.50	0	0	180	0	0	65	0	0
3	28.44	0	5.33	2099.33	180	0	192.67	0	17279.33	6100
4	28.44	360.89	27.17	655.78	180	0	143.44	0	34182.68	6100
5	80.00	0	24.77	0	113.34	0	159.92	0	37590.00	37590.00
6	48.78	43.83	21.18	0	96.76	0	0	65	33198.09	31060.26
7	16.80	1016.67	38.77	0	67.05	0	89.13	0	23181.38	6099.90
8	68.28	0	15.00	42.08	78.62	195	54.42	65	36958.81	17458.14
9	45.00	0	23.25	0	74.85	99.20	70.11	0	37078.91	29653.98
10	43.33	33.00	23.33	0	74.46	0	62.78	0	37040.00	35610.00

Figure 7.5 Estimated and reported profits during the planning sessions.

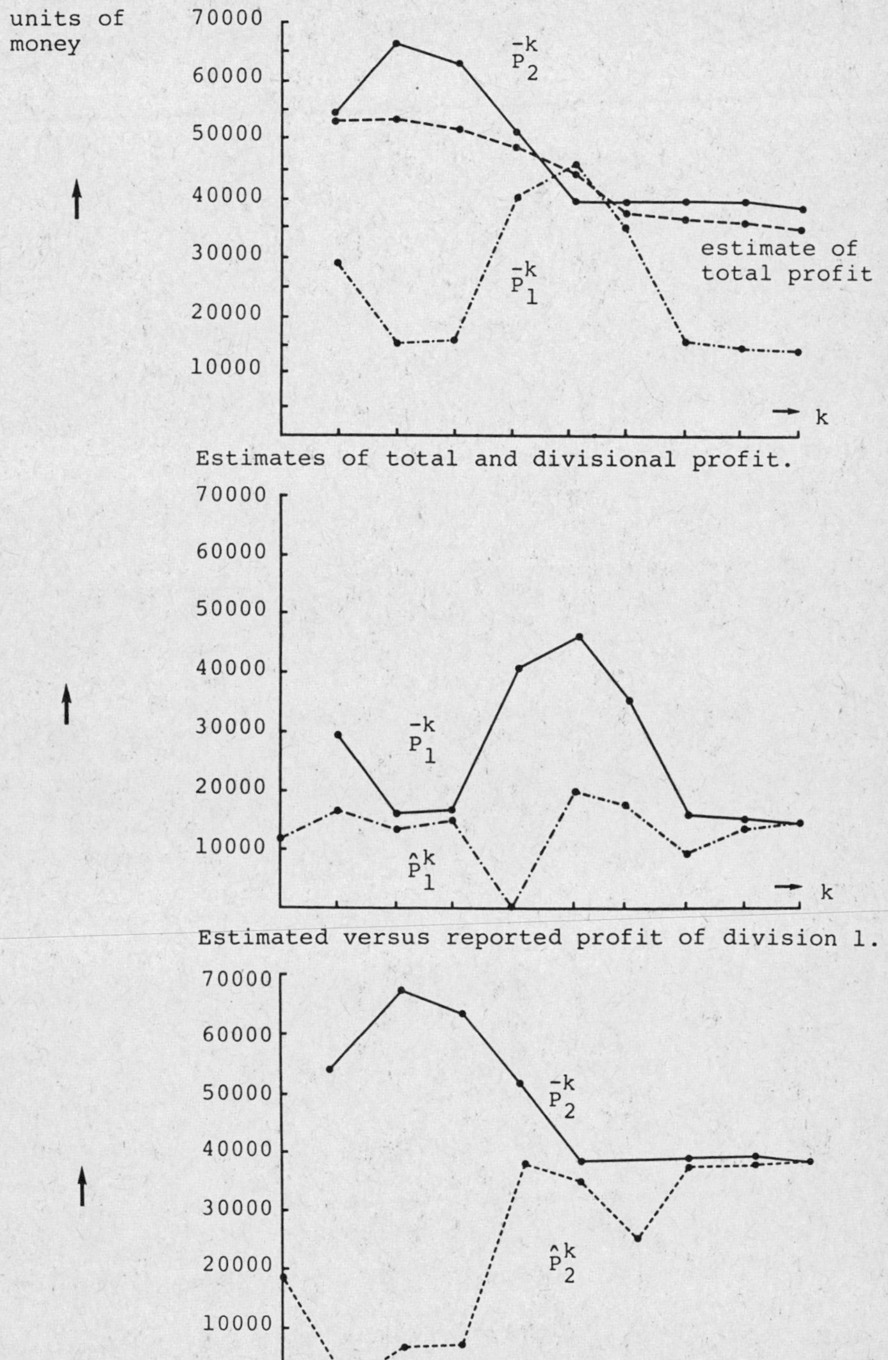

product, viz. $x_{2,1}(1)$, $x_{2,1}(2) > 0$ and $z_2(1) = 26.99 < 30$, while both CR-types are fully used up and no external TS is additionally bought. For the two divisions together the total number of decreased sales levels, mixing and additional external TS purchase is equal to $1 + (1+1) = 3$, while in the optimal situation this number is equal to 2 (cf. table 6.3-a).

The second example is concerned with additional external purchase of internally available TS. To this end we consider the divisional solutions in planning session 8. See table 7.6. Although division 2 is allocated TS_2 as well as TS_3, it buys additional TS_2 and TS_3 outside the firm: $y_2(2)$, $y_2(3) > 0$.

Finally, we present the divisional solutions of the last planning session (k=10). See table 7.6 and note the equivalence with table 6.3.

intermediate divisional activity plans			4th planning session		8th planning session		10th planning session	
DIVISIONS n=1,2			n=1	n=2	n=1	n=2	n=1	n=2
product type	technique	production volume						
1	1	$x_{n,1}(1)$	0	53.50	11.72	0	0	33.33
	2	$x_{n,1}(2)$	32.83	1.69	0	60	36.67	26.67
2	1	$x_{n,2}(1)$	38.87	56.79	21.15	60	41.85	60
	product type	sales level						
	1	$z_n(1)$	14.60	26.99	3.03	30	16.78	30
	2	$z_n(2)$	12.00	15.00	12.00	15	12.00	15
	TS type	external purchase						
	1	$y_n(1)$	53.26	0	20.78	0	59.49	0
	2	$y_n(2)$	0	0	0	1.38	0	0
	3	$y_n(3)$	0	0	0	5.58	0	0
units of CR not consumed	CR type							
		1	18.73	0	0	8.28	0	0
		2	0	0	21.56	0	0	0

Table 7.6: Tentative divisional activity plans during the planning procedure.

7.4. Cost allocations during the planning process

Up to now we have mainly been concerned with the two-level planning procedure that resolves the central unit problems concerning make-or-buy decisions, distributing internally produced TS to the divisions and coordinating the consumption of CR. This section completes the multilevel analysis with the incorporation of cost allocation mechanisms. In particular, the costs of producing certain TS-types internally have to be borne by consumers of these services. Similarly, the common costs, i.e. the costs incurred in the sector general services (GS), must be allocated. As in section 6.5, we cannot avoid the use of the word 'allocation' in its two different meanings: <u>allocation of input factors</u> (namely of CR and internal TS) and <u>allocation of costs</u> (namely costs of internal TS and common costs).

7.4.1. <u>Allocation of internal-TS costs</u>

We know that there are several good reasons for allocating the internal-TS costs associated with certain make-or-buy decisions (cf. sections 3.3.2 and 6.6.1). Because of the multilevel circumstances accounted for in this chapter, the central unit applies a planning procedure to generate information before decisions can actually be made. This procedure yields a sequence of temporary, tentative make-or-buy decisions and the central unit is permanently confronted with costs for internal TS. Therefore it will allocate these costs during the planning sessions in order to keep internal-TS consumers cost-conscious.

Because internal TS departments also deliver services to each other, costs will be allocated according to the reciprocal allocation method (cf. sections 3.3.2 and 6.5.1). This implies that in each planning session the central unit calculates a per-unit price for each internal TS-type and announces this price to the divisions together with their portions of each internal TS-type. The vector of prices is computed according to the formulas of section 6.5.1 with the only difference that the superscript 'opt' is replaced by 'k', which indicates the number of the current planning session. Thus the vector g^k of per-unit TS prices follows from:

$$g^k := (c^k + C^k \mathrm{diag}^{-1}[x_0^k; y_0^k])(I - D_0^k)^{-1} \tag{7.10}$$

Here x_0^k is the total amount of internally produced TS, y_0^k is the amount of external TS required in the production of x_0^k, and D_0^k is the input-output matrix of the TS alternative in the current planning session. The row vectors c^k and C^k contain the associated per-unit direct costs and fixed costs, respectively.

The allocation of internal-TS costs proceeds as follows. Let $g^k = (g^k(1),\ldots,g^k(M))$ be the (row) vector of per-unit prices. Let b_n^k be the vector of internal TS as allocated to division n. So division n obtains $b_n^k(m)$ units of internally produced TS_m. Now it is charged price $g^k(m)$ so that the division is allocated a cost equal to $g^k(m)b_n^k(m)$. The total costs allocated to division n are

$$\sum_{m=1}^{M} g^k(m)\bar{b}_n^k(m) = g^k\bar{b}_n^k \qquad (7.11)$$

However, the division has insight into the composition of the allocated costs because they are specified per TS-type.

To conclude, we analyse the influence of the incorporated cost allocation mechanism on the planning procedure. Instead of problem (7.2), each division now faces the following problem (recall that $\bar{b}_n^k \geqslant 0$)

$$
\begin{array}{lll}
\text{Maximize} & -c_n x_n - d y_n + p_n z_n - g^k b_n^k & \\[2mm]
\text{s.t.} & A_n x_n & \leqslant \bar{a}_n^k \\[2mm]
& B_n x_n - y_n & \leqslant \bar{b}_n^k \\[2mm]
& (I_n - D_n)x_n \quad - z_n & = 0 \\[2mm]
& z_n & \leqslant f_n \\[2mm]
x_n, y_n, z_n \geqslant 0 & & (7.12)
\end{array}
$$

which is formally equivalent to

$$
\begin{array}{lll}
\text{Maximize} & -c_n x_n - d y_n - g^k b_n + p_n z_n & \\[2mm]
\text{s.t.} & A_n x_n & \leqslant \bar{a}_n^k \\[2mm]
& B_n x_n - y_n - b_n & \leqslant 0 \\[2mm]
& b_n & = \bar{b}_n^k \\[2mm]
& (I_n - D_n)x_n \quad\quad - z_n & = 0 \\[2mm]
& z_n & \leqslant f_n \\[2mm]
x_n, y_n, z_n \geqslant 0 & & (7.13)
\end{array}
$$

The latter problem formally expresses that the division is obliged to use up the allocated amounts of internal TS while paying a per-unit price for each TS-type. As a result, the per-unit valuations of the obtained internal TS to be reported to the central unit will turn out to be lower, namely g^k, than the per-unit valuations that would have been obtained from solving the original divisional problem (7.2), i.e. in absence of the cost allocation mechanism. The central unit, knowing the deviation g^k, can easily reconstruct the correct per-unit valuations. Therefore the cost allocation mechanism does not distort the planning process.

In summary, internal-TS costs can be fully allocated during the planning procedure provided each division is obliged to use up its portion of the internally produced TS.

7.4.2. Common cost allocation

The allocation of internal-TS costs has been accomplished on a basis of usage and during the process of searching the production plan to be established, i.e. the planning sessions of the applied planning procedure. For common costs, there is no natural allocation basis and common cost allocation will take place after termination of the planning procedure, so at the end of the planning phase.

Similar to the 'complete information case' as treated in chapter six, we propose the application of an LP based cost allocation mechanism. The method requires the central unit to know shadow prices for CR. Secondly, the cost allocation method only allocates the common costs fully if they are smaller than the final valuation of the total CR capacity.

More precisely, let a_n^{opt}, b_n^{opt} $(n=1,\ldots,N)$ be the ultimate firm-wide optimal divisional portions of CR and internal TS respectively, as obtained at the end of the planning procedure. In other words, a_n^{opt} and b_n^{opt} are the CR and internal-TS allocations in the planning session that, subsequently, appeared to be the final planning session. Consider the divisional problem:

$$\text{Maximize} \quad -c_n x_n - dy_n + p_n z_n - g^{opt} b_n^{opt}$$

$$\text{s.t.} \quad A_n x_n \qquad\qquad\qquad\quad \leqslant a_n^{opt}$$

$$B_n x_n - y_n \qquad\qquad\qquad \leqslant b_n^{opt}$$

$$(I_n - D_n)x_n \qquad - z_n \qquad = 0$$

$$z_n \qquad\qquad \leqslant f_n$$

$$x_n, y_n, z_n \geqslant 0 \tag{7.14}$$

where g^{opt} is the vector of per-unit TS prices in this final planning session (cf. section 7.4.1.). Let x_n^{opt}, y_n^{opt}, z_n^{opt} denote an optimal solution to (7.14) with solution value $P_n^{opt} - g^{opt} b_n^{opt}$. This final divisional activity plan is also firm-wide optimal, as the division is allocated firm-wide optimal CR and TS portions. Furthermore, let $\hat{\pi}_n^{opt}$ denote the per-unit valuation of allocated CR (formally, an optimal dual variable associated with constraint $A_n x_n \leqslant a_n^{opt}$). Now $\hat{\pi}_n^{opt}$, $n = 1, \ldots, N$, which are reported by the divisions in the final planning session, can be used to allocate common costs as follows.

Let H denote the common costs, let $V(a) := H \leqslant \sum_{n=1}^{N} \hat{\pi}_n^{opt} a_n^{opt}$ and suppose $H \leqslant V(a)$. Then fraction h defined by $h := H/V(a)$ is smaller than 1. If division n is charged for consuming CR with a price equal to $h\pi_n^{opt}$, the original final activity plan remains optimal. Formally, if each division solves the modified problem:

$$\text{Maximize} \quad -(c_n + h\pi_n^{opt} A_n)x_n - dy_n + p_n z_n - g^{opt} b_n^{opt}$$

$$\text{s.t.} \quad A_n x_n \qquad\qquad\qquad\quad \leqslant a_n^{opt}$$

$$B_n x_n - y_n \qquad\qquad\qquad \leqslant b_n^{opt}$$

$$(I_n - D_n)x_n \qquad - z_n \qquad = 0$$

$$z_n \qquad\qquad \leqslant f_n$$

$$x_n, y_n, z_n \geqslant 0 \tag{7.15}$$

then x_n^{opt}, y_n^{opt}, z_n^{opt} is an optimal solution to (7.15) with solution value $P_n^{opt} - g^{opt}b_n^{opt} - h\hat{\pi}_n^{opt}a_n^{opt}$. The sum of these perturbed divisional profits is equal to $\sum_{n=1}^{N}(P_n^{opt} - g^{opt}b_n^{opt}) - H$. In other words, common costs H are allocated without distortion of total net profit

$$\sum_{n=1}^{N}(P_n^{opt} - g^{opt}b_n^{opt}) - H.$$

Common costs are thus allocated on the basis of the responses (π_n^{opt}) on the CR portions (a_n^{opt}), because these portions do not change anymore after termination of the procedure. Common costs cannot be allocated at any earlier point in the procedure, for CR portions as well as per-unit valuations change during the sessions of the planning procedure. For this reason, common costs are allocated at the end of the planning procedure, instead of during the procedure.

The proposed allocation methods can be applied to the numerical example as discussed in section 7.3.4.

The final price g^{opt} for TS appeared to be (cf. formula (7.10)):

$$g^{opt} = (165, \; 40 + 7000/84.39, \; 24 + 2000/99.34) \begin{bmatrix} 1 & 0.169 & 0.067 \\ 0 & 1.004 & 0.100 \\ 0 & 0.042 & 1.004 \end{bmatrix}$$

$$= (165, \; 122.95, \; 44.13)$$

The final portions and valuations of CR, i.e. a_n^{opt}, $\hat{\pi}_n^{opt}$, n=1,2, were (cf. table 7.4):

$$a_1^{opt} = (36.67, \; 36.67), \quad \hat{\pi}_1^{opt} = (191.98, \; 10.09)$$

$$a_2^{opt} = (43.33, \; 23.33), \quad \hat{\pi}_2^{opt} = (\; 33.00, \; \; 0)$$

so that $V(a) = 8839.80$. Suppose a common cost equal to 5000 has to be allocated. Now $h = 0.566$, and indeed the sum of the divisional profits is 5000 lower than in a situation with no common cost allocation.

7.5. <u>Summary</u>

On the basis of our general model of the firm we have investigated how to handle informational decentralization, being an important issue in two-level, divisionalized enterprises. The planning problem the central unit is faced with has been resolved by a resource-directive planning procedure. During the planning sessions information exchange has taken place between the central unit and the divisions in order to determine the portions of CR and internal TS of each division.

We have analysed intermediate divisional activity plans and, recalling the results of chapter six, compared them with the ultimate firm-wide situation. Furthermore attention was paid to the information contents of data as exchanged during the planning process.

The costs of internal production of TS can be allocated during the planning sessions. Common costs can be allocated at the end of the planning procedure. These final conclusions complete the multilevel analysis of the general model of the firm.

CHAPTER EIGHT

REVIEW AND EVALUATION

8.1. <u>Review of the text</u>

In the introductory chapter of this book we started with an informal
description of a general decentralized enterprise. We noted that the top
management is faced with complex planning problems while having incomplete information about subunits at the lower level in the organization.
We then formulated the aim of the book and discussed related contributions to the literature. In this section we will summarize how we
achieved the three goals in terms of which the aim of the book was expressed.

The first goal was to design a general model of the firm. The technological part was considered in chapter two in which we generalized the
input-output model of the firm. Products were allowed to have more than
one production technique. Secondly, we accounted for make-or-buy decisions with respect to technical services. Formally, the input-output
framework was transformed into a MIP formulation by an integral representation of all technology and TS alternatives.

In chapter three we treated an important financial issue, namely cost
allocation. The costs incurred in GS and TS departments have to be allocated, as these subunits do not supply to the outside market. We argued
that cost allocations can affect managerial behaviour and thus play a
role in multilevel decision-making. We concluded the chapter with the
incorporation of several organizational features and the statement of
the overall planning problem the firm is faced with.

The second goal was to obtain insight into the concept of multilevel
planning. This was achieved by analysing decomposition-based planning
procedures. Analogous to price and budget directed planning in existing
organizations we presented one price and one resource directive planning

procedure, based on the decomposition methods of Dantzig-Wolfe and Benders respectively.

The procedures can be adapted to various forms of informational decentralization. But decision-making authority is almost never decentralized: final decisions are made at the higher level in the organization.

In chapter five more sophisticated procedures were treated. We mixed price and resource directive characteristics. Special attention was paid to the way the central unit updates tentative prices and resource allocations. In this way we provided a theoretical basis for the simultaneous application of prices and budgets as observed in existing organizations.

In summary, we consciously built up the model of a two-level, divisionalized enterprise and then analysed decomposition-based planning procedures. The third goal of our work was to interpret the effects of such procedures in terms of the general model of the firm. Before this was accomplished, we investigated the planning problem of the firm from an overall point of view, i.e. not taking into account multilevel organizational features. The obtained provisional insight into the relationships between technology and TS alternatives functioned as a reference point when we subsequently decomposed the overall planning problem according to the underlying organization structure. In the latter approach, the central unit in the company deals with aggregated information on the divisions. During the planning process more alternatives are considered than ultimately applied in the final activity plans. However, the total amount of information processing is probably less than in the case of an overall solution approach.

8.2. Evaluation of the results

The main characteristic of the present book is its theoretical nature. We did not investigate a concrete practical problem existing in and borrowed from the real-world. Instead a general, theoretical basis for certain phenomena as observed in (particular areas in) reality was developed.

We have worked with mathematical techniques and model formulations which are not too advanced and which have limited complexity. For this reason the development as well as the final statement of results can be well understood. In this context we mention the assumption of linearity as used in the input-output and the mathematical programming models. Linearity is a most convenient and familiar way of thinking, not only in different theories but also in many practical rules of thumb.

The theoretical nature of the study can be further illustrated along the lines of our general model of the firm. We speak of a 'general' model, because several ideas on decision-making in a divisionalized enterprise are represented in a general, formal manner. Subsequently, the model of the firm functions as the basic economic framework or context. The final, overall planning problem, i.e. problem (3.6), is clearly an abstraction of reality. Nevertheless, it is impossible to be completely general: no model can integrate all relevant theories and still be easy to understand; no model can capture the integral reality of any multi-level enterprise.

At this point we wish to discuss the limitations of the theoretical research in more detail.

At first glance, one could be tempted to group the restrictions of the study into two separate classes, namely tool-oriented and problem-oriented restrictions. In this book tool-oriented limitations would refer to the particular choice of mathematical techniques and formulations (linearity, static and deterministic problems, one-dimensional objective functions). Problem-oriented restrictions are concerned with the chosen problem statement: they define or at least indicate boundaries of the problem field (informational decentralization, planning problems, two-level organizational structure). However, tool-oriented and problem-oriented restrictions are often interrelated. Therefore we now review the bounds between which problems have been investigated combined with the technical restrictions as implied or allowed by the research scope.

After having developed the general model of the firm, we focused our attention on the planning problem of the firm. In other words, one specific phase in the multilevel decision-making process was considered: the planning phase. We had at hand a relatively short-run planning problem, so that the problem formulations were static and deterministic. Furthermore we dealt mainly with informational decentralization, being an essential characteristic of planning in multilevel organizations. However, if subsequent stages in the decision-making process, such as implementation and control, would be considered, more dimensions of decentralization would 'inevitably' be noticed.

Secondly, we aimed at obtaining conceptual understanding of planning by prices and budgets. We provided a theoretical framework for coordination by transfer pricing and budgeting as observed in real-world organizations, particularly in divisionalized enterprises. As we wanted qualitative rather than quantitative insight, we could simply use linear models. The restriction to organizational structures with only two hierarchical levels is also a consequence of the theoretical nature of the study.

A more restrictive assumption is the assumption of 'harmony': central unit and divisional managers agree on the goal of the firm as a whole and there is no conflict of interests. Therefore it was reasonable to expect that every subunit contributes to the planning procedures as expected (e.g. reliable reporting of divisional profits, shadow prices and other data required by the central unit). The second consequence is that the ultimate decisions as made upon termination of the planning phase can be performed by the central unit. From a tool-oriented viewpoint the harmony assumption allowed the application of one-dimensional objective functions.

Although we presented a theoretical study, including several limitations of the research scope, the applied models and obtained results are probably reasonable descriptions, approximations of the real-world. Especially with respect to cost allocation, reality was approached quite closely. Indeed, cost allocation problems exist in organizations. A distinction between joint (or common) costs and costs of internally supplied technical services is most desirable. The linkage with coordination issues is obvious. We experienced that the incorporation of cost allocation mechanisms must be accomplished carefully. This explains why cost allocation is usually a problem in existing organizations.

The multilevel analysis of the model of the firm (cf. chapter seven) indicates that in the presence of make-or-buy decisions including avoidable fixed costs, a resource-directive system has to be applied. It seems very difficult to coordinate through prices when fixed costs have to be taken into account.

A third implication of our work is that the importance of information in planning situations is stressed and clarified. In our set-up the central unit has almost no information at the beginning of the planning phase. We have seen how the subsequent planning sessions enable the central unit to build up its information. It is reasonable to expect a somewhat richer description if a priori information is taken into account, i.e. the information the central unit possesses at the start of the planning procedure.

Within the context of our general model of the firm, which captures several realistic features, the study completely describes two-level planning in the presence of informational decentralization. Nevertheless the theory on multilevel decisions is extensive. The present book hopes to contribute to the exploration of this wide and challenging problem area.

In sections 2.3 and 2.4, we ended up with an LP and a MIP model of the firm, respectively. Furthermore, a number of properties of the formal models were discussed. This appendix is devoted to the formal proofs of the conjectured properties.

Consider problem (2.2), i.e.

$$\text{Minimize} \quad c_{prod} \, x_{prod}$$
$$\text{s.t.} \quad (I_\Phi - D_{\Phi\Phi}) \, x_{prod} = f$$
$$x_{prod} \geq 0 \tag{2.2}$$

It is required that $c_{prod} > 0$, $f > 0$ and $D_{\Phi\Phi} \geq 0$. Recall that a pure technology alternative is a technology alternative that applies exactly one technique per product. Now we have:

<u>Theorem 2.1:</u>

Assume that problem (2.2) is feasible for a certain final demand vector f that is strictly positive. Now the following conjectures are true:

1. A cost minimizing technology alternative exists that can produce f while using exactly one technique per product. Moreover, this pure technology alternative can produce every non-negative final demand at minimal costs.

2. Let D^* be the square matrix of the intermediate input coefficients and let c^* be the row vector of the direct cost coefficients of the pure technology alternative at hand. Now:

    2.a. Matrix $(I-D^*)$ is invertible and $(I-D^*)^{-1} \geq 0$.

    2.b. $v^* := c^* (I-D^*)^{-1}$ is dual optimal.

    2.c. v^* is dual optimal for every non-negative final demand.

Proof:

For a feasible solution x to problem (2.1), it holds that

$$\sum_{\psi=1}^{\Psi_{\tilde{\phi}}} x_{\tilde{\phi}}(\psi) = f_{\tilde{\phi}} + \sum_{\phi=1}^{\Phi} \sum_{\psi=1}^{\Psi_{\tilde{\phi}}} D_{\tilde{\phi}\phi}(\psi)\, x_{\phi}(\psi) > 0, \quad \tilde{\phi}=1,\ldots,\Phi,$$

as $D_{\phi\phi} \geqslant 0$ and $f_{\tilde{\phi}} > 0$. Thus for each $\tilde{\phi}$ at least one ψ exists such that $x_{\tilde{\phi}}(\psi) > 0$. This means that for each product at least one technique is applied. Each basic feasible solution, however, has at most Φ positive components. Hence it applies exactly one technique per product. The conclusion is that every basic feasible solution corresponds to a pure technology alternative that can produce the final demand. The associated basis matrix is of the form $(I-\hat{D})$. Here $\hat{D}$ is a square submatrix of $D_{\phi\phi}$, because exactly one technique per product is applied. Being a basis matrix, $(I-\hat{D})$ is non-singular. Moreover, $(I-\hat{D})\, x = f$ with $f > 0$ has a non-negative solution and from the theory of M-matrices it follows that $(I-\hat{D})^{-1} \geqslant 0$ (See Berman and Plemmons (1979, Ch. 6)).

Suppose that for some $f > 0$ problem (2.2) is feasible and recall $c_{prod} > 0$. It is evident that problem (2.2) has a finite optimum: its feasible region is closed and not empty while its solution value is bounded from below. One of the basic feasible solutions is optimal. Let $(I-D^{*})$ be the associated basis matrix. From standard LP theory, it follows that $v^{*} := c^{*}(I-D^{*})^{-1}$ is dual optimal.

Now consider (2.2) with an arbitrary final demand $\tilde{f} \geqslant 0$. The equation $(I-D^{*})\, x = \tilde{f}$ has a solution $\tilde{x}$, namely $\tilde{x} = (I-D^{*})^{-1} \tilde{f}$. Thanks to $\tilde{f} \geqslant 0$ and $(I-D^{*})^{-1} \geqslant 0$, we have $\tilde{x} \geqslant 0$. The vector $\tilde{x}$ is easily extended to a feasible solution of (2.1) with solution value $c^{*}\tilde{x}$. Furthermore v^{*} is still dual feasible as the dual feasible region has not changed, and has solution value $v^{*}\tilde{f} = c^{*}(I-D^{*})^{-1} \tilde{f} = c^{*}\tilde{x}$. Hence, we have found a primal-dual pair of solutions that is even optimal and still applies the original pure technology alternative. The vector v^{*} is dual optimal for every non-negative final demand. (End of proof)

In order to relax the assumption that every product faces a positive outside demand, we state and prove the following lemma:

<u>Lemma A1:</u>

Consider problem (2.2) with $f \geqslant 0$, $f \neq 0$. Suppose one has at hand a basic feasible solution that produces every product, i.e. for each ϕ there exists at least one ψ such that $x_\phi(\psi) > 0$. Then this basic solution applies exactly one technique per product.

Proof:

Problem (2.2) has Φ rows, so basic feasible solutions do not have more than Φ positive elements each. But because each product is produced, feasible solutions have at least Φ positive elements. Hence basic feasible solutions have exactly Φ positive elements and thus apply exactly one technique per product.   (End of proof)

Note that if for some $f > 0$ problem (2.2) is feasible, then the assumption as introduced in Lemma A1 holds for every basic feasible solution.

For the more general situation where at least one (but eventually not every) product faces a positive outside demand, we can state the following theorem.

<u>Theorem A1:</u>

Assume that problem (2.2) is feasible for a certain non-negative and non-zero final demand vector. Then a cost-minimizing solution exists that applies exactly one technique for each product that is actually produced.

Proof:

The problem at hand has a finite optimum for the same reasons as in the proof of Theorem 2.1. A cost minimizing solution that applies exactly one technique for each product actually produced can be determined as follows. Solve problem (2.2) with the simplex method. This yields an optimal basic solution. Now two possibilities exist:

1. For each ϕ at least one ψ exists such that $x_\phi(\psi) > 0$. From Lemma A1 it follows that we have found an optimal solution with the desired property.

2. At least one ϕ exists such that $x_\phi(\psi) = 0$ for all ψ, i.e. some product types are not produced at all. Now omit the coefficients and

variables associated to these products from the problem formulation and resolve the problem with the simplex method.

The process of solving and modifying the LP problem must be repeated until one has found a basic optimal solution to the latest version of (2.2) that obeys the condition as stated in Theorem A1. It can readily be transformed into an optimal solution of the starting version of (2.2) and indeed applies exactly one technique for products actually produced.

(End of proof)

We turn to the maximization model (2.3), i.e.

$$
\begin{aligned}
\text{Maximize} \quad & -c_{prod}\, x_{prod} + pz \\
\text{s.t.} \quad & (I_\phi - D_{\phi\phi})\, x_{prod} - z = 0 \\
& z \leqslant f \\
& x_{prod},\ z \geqslant 0
\end{aligned}
\tag{2.3}
$$

For this model a result similar to Lemma A1 can be proven.

<u>Lemma A2:</u>

Consider problem (2.3) with $f > 0$. Suppose one has at hand a basic feasible solution with the property: for each ϕ at least one ψ exists such that such that $x_\phi(\psi) > 0$. Then for this solution it holds that:

1. For each ϕ exactly one ψ exists with $x_\phi(\psi) > 0$;
2. For each ϕ either $z_\phi = 0$ or $z_\phi = f_\phi$.

Proof:

The basic optimal solution at hand has at least one $x_\phi(\psi) > 0$ for each ϕ, while z_ϕ and the slack variable corresponding to the constraint $z_\phi \leqslant f_\phi$ jointly deliver at least one positive element for each ϕ. However, basic feasible solutions to (2.3) cannot have more than 2Φ positive elements. Now property 1. and 2. easily follow. (End of proof)

Similar to the proof of Theorem A1, we can solve and modify problem (2.3) a number of times until we have obtained an optimal basic solution to the latest version of (2.3) that applies exactly one technique per product, i.e. obeys the condition as stated in Lemma A2. Therefore, without a complete proof, we state

<u>Theorem A2:</u>

Assume that (2.3) with $f > 0$ has a non-trivial optimum i.e. at least one $z_\phi > 0$. Then an optimal solution exists with the properties:

1. Exactly one technique is applied for each product actually produced;

2. Products are either sold maximally or not sold at all.

The MIP problems (2.6) and (2.8) account for make-or-buy decisions. We will prove that in an optimal situation each TS type is either produced internally or bought externally. First problem (2.6) is considered, i.e.

$$\text{Minimize} \qquad c_0 x_0 + dy + C\delta$$

$$\text{s.t.} \qquad (I - D_0)x_0 + y \qquad = b_0$$
$$x_0 \qquad - W\delta \leq 0$$
$$x_0, y \geq 0; \ \delta \ \text{0-1 vector} \tag{2.6}$$

It is required that $D_0 \geq 0$, $c_0 > 0$, $d > 0$, $C > 0$ and $b_0 > 0$. Furthermore $(I-D_0)^{-1}$ exists and is non-negative.

<u>Theorem A3:</u>

Consider problem (2.6) with $D_0 \geq 0$, c_0, d, C, $b_0 > 0$. Assume that $(I-D_0)^{-1} \geq 0$. Let δ^{opt} be part of an optimal solution $(x_0^{opt}, y^{opt}, \delta^{opt})$ to (2.6).

Now it holds that:

$$\delta^{opt}(m) = 1 \Rightarrow x_0^{opt}(m) > 0, \ y^{opt}(m) = 0 \tag{A.1-a}$$

$$\delta^{opt}(m) = 0 \Rightarrow x_0^{opt}(m) = 0, \ y^{opt}(m) > 0 \tag{A.1-b}$$

Proof:

If $\delta^{opt}(m) = 0$, then $x_0^{opt}(m) = 0$, because of $x_0^{opt}(m) - W \delta^{opt}(m) \leq 0$, and $y_0^{opt}(m) > 0$ because of $y^{opt}(m) = b_0(m) + (D_0 x_0^{opt})(m) > 0$.

If $\delta^{opt}(m) = 1$, then $x_0^{opt}(m) > 0$ because of $C(m) > 0$.

So the remaining statement to be proved is: if $\delta^{opt}(m) = 1$, then $y^{opt}(m) = 0$. The proof of this conjecture follows from certain properties of optimal basic solutions of a reformulated, equivalent version of (2.6).

Consider (2.6) with δ fixed, namely $\delta = \delta^{opt}$, and re-optimize the resulting continuous LP problem. For any optimal solution $(\hat{x}_0, \hat{y})$, it holds that $(\hat{x}_0, \hat{y}, \delta^{opt})$ is optimal to the original MIP problem (2.6), and thus $\hat{x}_0(m) > 0$ if $\delta^{opt}(m) = 1$ and $\hat{x}_0(m) = 0$, $\hat{y}(m) > 0$ if $\delta^{opt}(m) = 0$. As we know in advance which elements of x_0 will turn out to be positive and which will be zero in an optimal solution, we rewrite the constraints of the continuous LP problem (i.e. (2.6) with $\delta = \delta^{opt}$) in the following way:

$$(I - D_0)\begin{bmatrix} \tilde{x}_0 \\ \hline 0 \end{bmatrix} + \begin{bmatrix} \tilde{y} \\ \hline \approx \\ y \end{bmatrix} = b_0,$$
$$\tilde{x}_0, \tilde{y}, \overset{\approx}{y} \geqslant 0 \tag{*}$$

Now the constraints $x_0 \leqslant W \delta^{opt}$ have become redundant. In fact we are dealing with the continuous LP problem:

$$\text{Minimize } \overset{\sim}{\tilde{c}}x_0 + \overset{\sim}{\tilde{d}}y + \overset{\approx}{\tilde{d}}y \quad \text{s.t. } (*) \tag{A.2}$$

Note that the (constant) term $C\delta^{opt}$ is omitted from the objective function.

Basic feasible solutions to this LP problem have at most M positive elements. Optimal solutions must have $\tilde{x}_0 > 0$, $\overset{\approx}{y} > 0$ and this yields already M positive elements. Hence optimal basic solutions have exactly M positive elements, viz. the elements of $\tilde{x}_0$ and $\overset{\approx}{y}$, and the $\tilde{y}$-part must be equal to zero. Now suppose that no unbounded solution exists that attains the finite optimal solution value. Then each optimal solution to (A.2) can be written as a convex combination of the optimal basic solutions, and the property $\tilde{y} = 0$ is maintained.

Indeed, the feasible region of (*) is bounded. Returning to the original notation as used in problem (2.6), we note that $x_0 = (I-D_0)^{-1} b_0 - (I-D_0)^{-1}y$, $b_0 > 0$, $y \geqslant 0$. Hence $0 \leqslant x_0 \leqslant (I-D_0)^{-1} b_0$. Secondly $x_0 + y = D_0 x_0 + b_0$ with $D_0 \geqslant 0$. So x_0 is bounded and this implies the boundedness of y.

The conclusion is that optimal solutions to (A.2) must have $\tilde{y} = 0$. In terms of problem (2.6) with $\delta = \delta^{opt}$, this means that $y^{opt}(m) = 0$ whenever $\delta^{opt}(m) = 1$.

(End of proof)

We conclude the appendix with a theorem concerning the MIP problem (2.8), i.e.

$$\text{Maximize} \quad -c_{prod}\, x_{prod} + pz - c_0 x_0 - dy - C\delta$$

$$\text{s.t.} \quad (I_\phi - D_{\phi\phi})\, x_{prod} - z = 0$$

$$z \leq f$$

$$- D_{M\phi}\, x_{prod} + (I - D_0)x_0 + y = 0$$

$$x_0 - W\delta \leq 0$$

$$x_{prod},\ z,\ x_0,\ y \geq 0$$

$$\delta \ \text{0-1 vector} \tag{2.8}$$

Problem (2.8) resulted from putting together (2.3) and (2.6), so that the following theorem is valid.

Theorem A4:

Assume that problem (2.8) with c_{prod}, c_0, d, C, f > 0 has a non-trivial optimum, i.e. at least one $z_\phi > 0$. Then an optimal solution exist with the properties:

1. Exactly one technique is applied for each product actually produced;
2. Products are either sold maximally or not sold at all;
3. Each TS type that is required is either produced internally or bought externally.

APPENDIX B: appendix to CHAPTER THREE

This appendix is devoted to the mathematical background of the allocation method as presented in section 3.3.3. It is thus concerned with the LP problem

Maximize px

s.t. $\quad Ax \leqslant a$

$\quad\quad\ Bx \leqslant b$

$\quad\quad\ \ x \geqslant 0$ $\hspace{8cm}$ (3.4)

and its dual

Minimize $\pi a + \rho b$

s.t. $\quad \pi a + \rho b \geqslant p$

$\quad\quad\quad\ \pi,\rho \geqslant 0$ $\hspace{8cm}$ (B.1)

Let $(\bar{x}; \bar{\pi}, \bar{\rho})$ be primal-dual optimal to (3.4) and (B.1) respectively with solution value OPT. We assume $0 < \text{OPT} < \infty$.

Take $h_1, h_2 \leqslant 1$ and consider the following perturbed version of (3.4):

Maximize $(p - h_1 \bar{\pi} A - h_2 \bar{\rho} B)x$

s.t. $\quad\quad\quad\quad Ax \leqslant a$

$\quad\quad\quad\quad\quad\ Bx \leqslant b$

$\quad\quad\quad\quad\quad\ \ x \geqslant 0$ $\hspace{7cm}$ (B.2)

Now we have:

<u>Theorem B.1:</u>

Consider problem (B.2) with $h_1, h_2 \leqslant 1$ and $(\bar{\pi}, \bar{\rho})$ optimal to (B.1). Let $\bar{x}$ be optimal to (3.4). Then:

1. $\bar{x}$ is also optimal to (B.2);

2. The optimal solution value of (B.2) is $\text{OPT} - h_1 \bar{\pi} a - h_2 \bar{\rho} b$;

3. $((1-h_1)\bar{\pi}, (1-h_2)\bar{\rho})$ is dual optimal to (B.2).

<u>Proof:</u>

It is clear that $\bar{x}$ is primal feasible. Furthermore $((1-h_1)\bar{\pi},\ (1-h_2)\bar{\rho})$ is dual feasible, as $(1-h_1)\bar{\pi} > 0$, $(1-h_2)\bar{\rho} > 0$, due to h_1, $h_2 < 1$, and

$$(1-h_1)\bar{\pi}A + (1-h_2)\bar{\rho}B = \bar{\pi}A + \bar{\rho}B - h_1\bar{\pi}A - h_2\bar{\rho}B > p - h_1\bar{\pi}A - h_2\bar{\rho}B$$

Because of $\bar{\pi}(A\bar{x}-a) = 0$ and $\bar{\rho}(B\bar{x}-b) = 0$, the objective function value of $\bar{x}$ is equal to $p\bar{x} - h_1\bar{\pi}a - h_2\bar{\rho}b$. On the other hand, $((1-h_1)\bar{\pi},\ (1-h_2)\bar{\rho})$ has solution value $(1-h_1)\bar{\pi}a + (1-h_2)\bar{\rho}b = \bar{\pi}a + \bar{\rho}b - h_1\bar{\pi}a - h_2\bar{\rho}b$. Now recall that $OPT = p\bar{x} = \bar{\pi}a + \bar{\rho}b$. It follows that the primal and dual solution value are equal.

Conclusion:

$\bar{x}$ and $((1-h_1)\bar{\pi},\ (1-h_2)\bar{\rho})$ are primal-dual feasible with equal solution value, viz. $OPT - h_1\bar{\pi}a - h_2\bar{\rho}b$, and are thus primal-dual optimal.

(End of proof)

C.1. <u>Derivation of the price-directive planning procedure following Dantzig-Wolfe</u>

The price-directive planning procedure as discussed in section 4.3 is based on the decomposition method of Dantzig-Wolfe (see Dantzig (1963, ch. 23)). In this part of the appendix, the mathematical derivation of the procedure is given under a reasonable set of assumptions.

The problem to be solved is the following block-angular LP problem, which is presumed to be feasible.

$$
\begin{aligned}
\text{Maximize} \quad & p_1 x_1 + \ldots + p_N x_N \\
\text{s.t.} \quad & A_1 x_1 + \ldots + A_N x_N \leq a \\
& Q_1 x_1 \qquad\qquad\quad \leq q_1 \\
& \qquad \ddots \qquad\quad \vdots \\
& \qquad\qquad Q_N x_N \leq q_N \\
& x_1, \ldots, x_N \geq 0
\end{aligned}
\tag{4.1}
$$

For notational convenience, it is assumed that the divisional feasible regions $F_n := \{ x_n \mid Q_n x_n \leq q_n, \ x_n \geq 0 \}$, $n=1,\ldots,N$, are bounded. Expressing each x_n as a convex combination of the extreme points x_n^i, $i=1,\ldots,S_n$, of F_n, leads to the following reformulated version of (4.1):

$$
\text{Maximize} \quad \sum_{n=1}^{N} \sum_{i=1}^{S_n} p_n^i \lambda_n^i
$$

$$
\text{s.t.} \quad \sum_{n=1}^{N} \sum_{i=1}^{S_n} A_n^i \lambda_n^i \leq a
$$

$$
\sum_{i=1}^{S_n} \lambda_n^i = 1 \ , \ n = 1,\ldots,N
$$

$$
\text{all } \lambda_n^i \geq 0
\tag{C.1}
$$

Here $p_n^i := p_n x_n^i$ and $A_n^i := A_n x_n^i$ $(i=1,\ldots,S_n, \ n=1,\ldots,N)$. Problem (C.1), to be referred to as the full master problem, is again an LP problem, with the λ_n^i as variables. In comparison with problem (4.4) we see that in (C.1) all extreme points of each F_n are specified. Therefore we have S_n instead of $\bar{S}_n$.

The algorithm to be presented solves (C.1) rather than (4.1). In comparison with the original formulation, the full master problem has only a few rows, but could have a large number of columns. The whole set of columns is not specified in advance; columns will be generated when they are needed.

Suppose that, at some stage in the solution process, a subset of all columns of the problem is available. The LP problem based on this subset of columns, i.e. problem (4.4), is called the restricted master problem and is optimized. The optimal solution of the current restricted master problem is also optimal to the full master problem if the relative cost coefficient (rcc) of every non-basic column, i.e. every column not specified in the restricted version of the master problem, is non-positive. Otherwise, the column with the largest positive rcc will be added to the restricted master problem. It should be noted that this solution strategy has much resemblance to the ordinary simplex method for linear programming problems (see e.g. Lasdon (1970, section 1.2)). The essential difference is that we do not have a complete specification of the non-basic columns here.

The algorithm proceeds as follows. Solve the restricted master problem with a certain subset of columns. Let $\bar{\pi}_0$ be the optimal dual multiplier associated with the inequality constraints and let $\bar{\omega}_n$, $n = 1,\ldots,N$, be the optimal dual multipliers associated with the equality constraints. Now the rcc of the column corresponding to the extreme point x_n^i is given by the expression

$$\mathrm{rcc}_n^i := p_n^i - \bar{\pi}_0 A_n^i - \bar{\omega}_n = (p_n - \bar{\pi}_0 A_n)x_n^i - \bar{\omega}_n \qquad (C.2)$$

As already noted, the current solution to the restricted master problem is also optimal to the full master problem if for all n every $\mathrm{rcc}_n^i < 0$.

The optimality condition is checked by solving each of the following divisional problems:

Maximize $(p_n - \bar{\pi}_0 A_n) x_n$

s.t. $\quad\quad\quad Q_n x_n \leqslant q_n$

$\quad\quad\quad\quad\quad x_n \geqslant 0$ $\quad\quad\quad\quad\quad\quad\quad\quad\quad\quad\quad\quad$ (4.3)

Denote the optimum value by $\hat{P}_n$. Because (4.2) is feasible and the set F_n is bounded, $\hat{P}_n$ is finite. This finite optimum is attained at an extreme point $\hat{x}_n^i$, and $\hat{P}_n = (p_n - \bar{\pi}_0 A_n) \hat{x}_n^i$. In case $\hat{P}_n - \bar{\omega}_n > 0$, the column $((A_n \hat{x}_n^i)', 0, \ldots, 0, 1, 0, \ldots, 0)'$ should be added to the restricted master problem, with associated objective function coefficient $p_n \hat{x}_n^i$. In case $\hat{P}_n - \bar{\omega}_n \leqslant 0$, the n-th divisional problem does not deliver a new column for the restricted master problem.

If, for each n, $\hat{P}_n - \bar{\omega}_n \leqslant 0$, then no columns exist that not already have been specified in the restricted master problem and that can improve the current optimal solution to the restricted master problem. So this solution is also optimal to the full master problem and the algorithm is terminated. If, on the other hand, columns are to be added for some n, a new iteration is necessary with at least one and at most N new columns added to the restricted master problem. Assuming no degeneracies, an optimum will be reached in a finite number of iterations, for the full master problem (4.4) is an ordinary LP problem, with a finite number of columns.

Two final remarks are in order. At each stage in the solution process, the solution to the current restricted master problem (denoted by $\bar{\lambda}_n^i$, $i = 1, \ldots, \bar{S}_n$, $n = 1, \ldots, N$) can be transformed into a solution of the original problem (4.1), viz. by the formula

$$\bar{x}_n := \sum_{i=1}^{\bar{S}_n} \bar{\lambda}_n^i x_n^i, \quad n = 1, \ldots, N \quad\quad\quad\quad\quad (4.5)$$

This holds particularly for the optimal solution to the full master problem. Secondly, we mention the assumption that, upon initialization of the algorithm, a set of columns of the restricted master problem is available such that the problem has a feasible solution. Then it is possible to optimize the restricted master problem and obtain a set of dual multipliers. Further (technical) considerations concerning this assump-

tion, which is not really restrictive, can be found in Dirickx et al.
(1979, p. 46).

C.2. <u>Derivation of the resource-directive planning procedure following Benders</u>

In this part of the appendix, the resource-directive planning procedure
of section 4.4 is mathematically derived.

Again, we start our exposition with a block-angular LP problem, which
is presumed to have a finite optimum. Contrary to section C.1, we use
the symbols B_n and b for the common constraints:

$$
\begin{aligned}
\text{Maximize } & p_1 x_1 + \ldots + p_N x_N \\
\text{s.t. } \quad & B_1 x_1 + \ldots + B_N x_N \leq b \\
& Q_1 x_1 \qquad\qquad\qquad \leq q_1 \\
& \qquad \ddots \qquad\qquad\quad \vdots \\
& \qquad\qquad\quad Q_N x_N \leq q_N \\
& \quad x_1, \ldots, x_N \geq 0
\end{aligned}
\tag{4.6}
$$

Problem (4.6) can be rewritten as follows:

$$
\begin{aligned}
\text{Maximize } & p_1 x_1 + \qquad\quad \ldots + p_N x_N \\
\text{s.t. } \quad & B_1 x_1 - b_1 \qquad\qquad\qquad\qquad \leq 0 \\
& Q_1 x_1 \qquad\qquad\qquad\qquad\qquad \leq q_1 \\
& \qquad \ddots \qquad\qquad\qquad\qquad \vdots \\
& \qquad\qquad\quad B_N x_N - b_n \leq 0 \\
& \qquad\qquad\quad Q_N x_N \qquad \leq q_n \\
& b_1 + \ldots \qquad\qquad + b_N = b \\
& \quad x_1, \ldots, x_N \geq 0
\end{aligned}
\tag{4.7}
$$

Problems (4.6) and (4.7) are equivalent in the sense that (4.6) has an
(optimal) solution if (4.7) has an (optimal) solution, and reversely.
See also Dirickx and Jennergren (1979, p. 66).

Roughly speaking, the idea is to solve (4.7) with fixed values of b_n,
say $\bar{b}_n$, where $\bar{b}_1 + \ldots + \bar{b}_N = b$. By using information from the dual version of (4.7), a better partitioning of CR vector b is computed. This
process is repeated until it is not possible to improve the partitioning
of b.

At this point in the presentation, it is worthwile to note that Benders (1962) developed his partitioning method for a more general class of problems than (4.7), namely problems of the form:

$$\text{Maximize } px + f(b)$$
$$\text{s.t.} \quad Ax + F(b) \leqslant a$$
$$x \geqslant 0$$
$$b \in U \qquad\qquad (C.4)$$

Here f is a scalar valued and F is a vector valued function. U is an arbitrary subset of $\mathbb{R}^s$, where $\mathbb{R}^s$ denotes the s-dimensional Euclidian space. Moreover the b variables are not restricted to be continuous. In chapter seven, we will utilize this property of the Benders method: 0-1 variables will occur in the b-part of the variables. Now we return to the solution of (4.7).

For a given partitioning $(b_1,\ldots,b_N)$, problem (4.7) decomposes into N separate problems, which we write in the following form ($n=1,\ldots,N$):

$$\text{Maximize } P_n$$
$$\text{s.t.} \quad P_n - p_n x_n \leqslant 0$$
$$B_n x_n \leqslant b_n$$
$$Q_n x_n \leqslant q_n$$
$$x_n \geqslant 0 \qquad\qquad (4.8)$$

Instead of searching a combination (x_n, P_n) that optimizes (4.8), we proceed the other way round: given some (b_n, P_n), is there a vector x_n such that $P_n \leqslant p_n x_n$, $B_n x_n \leqslant b_n$, $Q_n x_n \leqslant q_n$, $x_n \geqslant 0$?

Below, necessary and sufficient conditions for b_n and P_n are stated that guarantee the existence of this x_n. They can be derived by applying Farkas' lemma (See e.g. Dirickx and Jennergren (1979, p. 57)). The next problem is then to choose b_n and maximal P_n, subject to these conditions and such that $b_1 + \ldots + b_N = b$.

If we assume that each b_n is taken from the set

$U_n := \{b_n \mid \exists_{x_n} (B_n x_n \leqslant b_n, Q_n x_n \leqslant q_n, x_n \geqslant 0)\}$, the conditions meant above

are

$$P_n \leqslant \rho_n^j b_n + \eta_n^j q_n, \quad j = 1,\ldots,S_n, \tag{C.5}$$

where (ρ_n^j, η_n^j), $j = 1,\ldots,S_n$ denote the extreme points of the dual feasible region $\{(\rho_n,\eta_n) \mid \rho_n B_n + \eta_n Q_n \geqslant P_n; \rho_n, \eta_n \geqslant 0\}$.

(Assumption $b_n \in U_n$ may be unrealistic. However, it can easily be dropped, but this would induce notational complications. For the more general case, we refer to the literature, e.g. Dirickx and Jennergren (1979, section 3.3.6)).

Thus, we have arrived at the following full master problem:

Maximize $P_1 + \ldots + P_N$

s.t. $\quad P_n \leqslant \rho_n^j b_n + \eta_n^j q_n, \quad j = 1,\ldots,S_n; \; n = 1,\ldots,N$

$$(b_1,\ldots,b_N) \in U \tag{C.6}$$

where $U := \{(b_1,\ldots,b_N) \mid b_1 + \ldots + b_N = b, \; b_n \in U_n, \; n = 1,\ldots,N\}$. The algorithm to be presented solves (C.6) rather than (4.7). The LP problem (C.6) may have many restrictions, because the number of extreme points can be very large. On the other hand, only a small fraction of the constraints will be binding at optimality. The algorithm generates constraints successively, only when they are needed.

Suppose that, at some stage in the solution process, a subset of all rows of the problem has been generated. The problem based on this subset of rows is called the relaxed master problem and is optimized. The optimal solution of the current relaxed master problem is also globally optimal, if this solution appears to obey the constraints not specified in the current relaxed problem.

The algorithm proceeds as follows. Each iteration starts with the solution of a relaxed version of (C.6), so with a certain subset of rows. Let $(\bar{P}_1,\ldots,\bar{P}_N, \bar{b}_1,\ldots,\bar{b}_N)$ denote the solution of the relaxed master problem. This solution is optimal for (C.6), if and only if each of the constraints in (4.12) is satisfied. For every n, the most unsatisfied constraint can be found by checking

$$\bar{P}_n > \min \{\rho_n^j b_n + \eta_n^j q_n \mid j=1,\ldots,S_n\} \qquad (C.7)$$

Such an index can be determined by solving the dual divisional problems $(n=1,\ldots,N)$:

Minimize $\rho_n b_n + \eta_n q_n$
s.t. $\rho_n B_n + \eta_n Q_n \geqslant p_n$
$$\rho_n,\eta_n \geqslant 0 \qquad (C.8)$$

Denote the optimum value by $\hat{P}_n$. The primal version of (C.8) is feasible as $b_n \in U_n$, so $\hat{P}_n > -\infty$. Secondly, $\hat{P}_n < +\infty$ because we assumed that the original problem has a bounded optimum. The finite optimum $\hat{P}_n$ is attained at an extreme point, say $(\hat{\rho}_n^j, \hat{\eta}_n^j)$. In case $\hat{P}_n < \bar{P}_n$, the constraint

$$P_n < \hat{\rho}_n^j b_n + \hat{\eta}_n^j q_n$$

is added to the relaxed master problem. Note that this inequality is equivalent with (4.9), as $\eta_n^j q_n = \hat{P}_n - \hat{\rho}_n^j \bar{b}_n$ and superscript j was suppressed in (4.9). If $\hat{P}_n \geqslant \bar{P}_n$, for each n, the solution to the current version of the relaxed master problem obeys (C.5). Then we have found a solution which is optimal to the full master problem (C.6), too, and the algorithm is terminated. The primal solutions to (C.8), say $\hat{x}_n$ $(n=1,\ldots,N)$ are now globally optimal. If, on the other hand, constraints have been added, a new iteration will be necessary with the augmented subset of constraints.

The algorithm converges in a finite number of iterations, as the full master problem (C.6) has a finite number of constraints.

D.1. Proof of Theorem 5.1

Consider the problem

Maximize px

s.t. $\quad Ax \leqslant a$

$\quad\quad\ Bx \leqslant b$

$\quad\quad\ x \geqslant 0$ $\hfill$ (D.1)

with optimal solution $\hat{x}$. Let $\hat{\pi}, \hat{\rho}$ solve the dual problem

Minimize $\quad \pi a + \rho b$

s.t. $\quad\quad \pi A + \rho B \geqslant p$

$\quad\quad\quad\quad \pi, \rho \geqslant 0$ $\hfill$ (D.2)

Then it holds that $\hat{\pi}(A\hat{x}-a) = 0$, and $\hat{x}$ is an optimal solution to

Maximize $(p-\hat{\pi}A)x$

s.t. $\quad\quad Bx \leqslant b$

$\quad\quad\quad x \geqslant 0$ $\hfill$ (D.3)

Define:

$$L(x,\pi) := px - \pi(Ax-a), \quad Bx \leqslant b, \ x \geqslant 0, \ \pi \geqslant 0.$$

We will prove that $(\hat{x},\hat{\pi})$ is a saddle point of $L(x,\pi)$, i.e.

$$L(x,\hat{\pi}) \leqslant L(\hat{x},\hat{\pi}) \leqslant L(\hat{x},\pi) \text{ for } \pi \geqslant 0 \text{ and all } x \text{ with } Bx \leqslant b, \ x \geqslant 0 \quad (D.4)$$

As $\hat{x}$ solves (D.3), we have $(p-\hat{\pi}A)x \leqslant (p-\hat{\pi}A)\hat{x}$, so $L(x,\hat{\pi}) \leqslant L(\hat{x},\hat{\pi})$.
Secondly, $\hat{\pi}(A\hat{x}-a) = 0$ whereas $-\pi(A\hat{x}-a) \geqslant 0$, so $L(\hat{x},\hat{\pi}) \leqslant L(\hat{x},\pi)$.
Summarizing, we have shown that if (D.1) has an optimal solution $\hat{x}$, then
some $\hat{\pi} \geqslant 0$ exists such that $(\hat{x},\hat{\pi})$ is a saddlepoint of $L(x,\pi)$.

Reversely, if $L(x,\pi)$ has a saddlepoint $(\hat{x},\hat{\pi})$ then $\hat{x}$ solves the original problem (A.1). This statement is true for any mathematical programming problem, see Lasdon (1970), p. 85).

D.2. Further relaxation of problem (5.20)

We will show that for each $k = 1,\ldots,r$ the following inequality holds:

$$P_n(\pi,b_n^k) \geqslant P_n(\pi^k,b_n^k) + (\pi^k-\pi)A_n\hat{x}_n^k \tag{D.5}$$

with (obviously) equality for $\pi = \pi^k$.

Recall the definition of $P_n(\pi,b_n)$ (page 62). For all x_n satisfying $B_n x_n \leqslant b_n^k$, $x_n \in F_n$, it holds that

$$P_n(\pi,b_n^k) \geqslant (p_n-\pi^k A_n)x_n + (\pi^k-\pi)A_n x_n$$

In particular

$$P_n(\pi,b_n^k) \geqslant (p_n-\pi^k A_n)\hat{x}_n^k + (\pi^k-\pi)A_n\hat{x}_n^k$$

which is equivalent to

$$P_n(\pi,b_n^k) \geqslant P_n(\pi^k,b_n^k) + (\pi^k-\pi)A_n\hat{x}_n^k.$$

Now that we have proved (D.5), it easily follows that

$$\sum_{n=1}^{N} P_n(\pi,b_n^k) + \pi a \geqslant P_{sum}^k + (\pi-\pi^k)\Delta_a^k \tag{D.6}$$

where $P_{sum}^k := \sum_{n=1}^{N} P_n(\pi^k,b_n^k) + \pi^k a$, $\Delta_a^k := a - \sum_{n=1}^{N} A_n\hat{x}_n^k$.

(D.6) is precisely inequality (5.23).

D.3. A convergence proof for the algorithm as presented in section 5.3.1.

In this section we will prove convergence of the algorithm as presented in section 5.3.1. Two more assumptions are required. After the proof, a sufficient condition for one of them is given.

Theorem:

If we assume that

1. the sequence $(\pi^r)_1^\infty$, is bounded,
2. the $\hat{\rho}_n^r$ are uniformly bounded,

then the algorithm of section 5 converges in the sense that

$$w^r - v^r \downarrow 0, \quad r \to \infty.$$

Proof:

We already know that $v^r \leqslant v^{r+1} \leqslant v(D) = w(P) \leqslant w^{r+1} \leqslant w^r$. In the sequel we will prove that $w^r - v^r \downarrow 0$ on a subset of indices. Of course, this implies that

$$\lim_{r \to \infty} v^r = v(D) = w(P) = \lim_{r \to \infty} w^r.$$

The reasoning proceeds as follows.

The sequence $(\pi^r, b_1^r, \ldots, b_n^r)_1^\infty$ converges on a subset of indices, as the π^r and all b_n^r come from bounded sets. (The boundedness of U follows from the compactness of each F_n and the global restriction $\sum_{n=1}^N b_n \leqslant b$) The convergent sub-sequences are denoted by

$$(\pi^{r_s})_{s=1}^\infty \quad \text{and} \quad (b_n^{r_s})_{s=1}^\infty, \quad n = 1, \ldots, N.$$

As $v^{r_s+1} \geqslant P_{sum}^{r_s} + (\pi^{r_s+1} - \pi^{r_s}) \Delta_a^{r_s}$

and $w^{r_s+1} \leqslant P_{sum}^{r_s} + \sum_{n=1}^N \hat{\rho}_n^{r_s} (b_n^{r_s+1} - b_n^{r_s})$,

we have

$$0 \leqslant w^{r_{s+1}} - v^{r_{s+1}} \leqslant (\pi^{r_{s+1}} - \pi^{r_s}) \Delta_a^{r_s} + \sum_{n=1}^{N} \hat{\rho}_n^{r_s} (b_n^{r_{s+1}} - b_n^{r_s})$$

For $s \to \infty$, the right-hand side of this expression converges to 0 as $\Delta_a^{r_s}$ and $\hat{\rho}_n^{r_s}$ are bounded. (The boundedness of $\Delta_a^{r_s}$ is simply due to the boundedness of the sets F_n, $n=1,\ldots,N$.) Hence

$$v^{r_s} - w^{r_s} \downarrow 0 \, , \quad s \to \infty \qquad\qquad \text{(End of proof)}$$

Finally, we present a sufficient condition for assumption 1 in the theorem. Suppose that there exists a known, feasible solution $\tilde{x}_1,\ldots,\tilde{x}_n$ such that $\sum_{n=1}^{N} A_n \tilde{x}_n < a$. The knowledge of this 'interior point' can be used as follows. From (5.14) it is clear that

$$v(D) \geqslant \min_{\pi \geqslant 0} L(x,\pi) \text{ for every } \underline{\text{fixed}} \text{ feasible } x$$

As a consequence, each (D_r) remains to be a relaxed dual problem if we add the constraint $v \geqslant L(\tilde{x},\pi)$ to (D_r) $(r = 1,2,\ldots)$. With respect to the algorithm, we suppose that, upon initialitation, (D_r) with $r = 0$ has only one constraint, viz.

$$v \geqslant \sum_{n=1}^{N} p_n \tilde{x}_n + \pi(a - \sum_{n=1}^{N} A_n \tilde{x}_n)$$

which will be maintained throughout the subsequent iterations. An immediate consequence of this modification is that the sequence $(\pi^r)_1^\infty$ will be bounded. To prove this, define: $\pi_i^r :=$ the i-th component of π^r; $\tilde{P} := \sum_{n=1}^{N} p_n \tilde{x}_n$; $\tilde{\Delta}_i :=$ the i-th component of $a - \sum_{n=1}^{N} A_n \tilde{x}_n$. Now we have:

$$0 \leqslant \pi_i^{r+1} \tilde{\Delta}_i \leqslant \sum_i \pi_i^{r+1} \tilde{\Delta}_i \leqslant v^r - \tilde{P} \leqslant v(D) - \tilde{P}$$

so $0 \leqslant \pi_i^{r+1} \leqslant (v(D) - \tilde{P})/(\tilde{\Delta}_i)$, as $\tilde{\Delta}_i > 0$

In other words, all future π_i^r are bounded.

In this appendix we will prove Theorems 6.1 and 6.2 as presented in section 6.2. We introduce a different, more compact MIP problem which will appear to be equivalent to problem (6.1) in a certain sense. Observe that the constraints

$$
\begin{aligned}
B_1 x_1 - y_1 - b_1 & \leq 0 \\
\ddots & \quad \vdots \\
B_N x_N - y_N - b_N & \leq 0 \\
b_1 \cdots \qquad + b_N - b_0 & = 0 \\
b_0 - (I - D_0)x_0 - y_0 & = 0
\end{aligned}
$$

as present in problem (6.1) can be replaced by

$$
\sum_{n=1}^{N} B_n x_n - (I - D_0)x_0 - y \leq 0
$$

where $y := y_0 + y_1 + \cdots + y_N$. In this way the variables $b_0, b_1, \ldots, b_N$ and $y_0, y_1, \ldots, y_N$ are eliminated. Omitting the constraints $b_0 - W\delta \leq 0$ we obtain the following MIP problem:

$$
\begin{aligned}
\text{Maximize} \quad & \sum_{n=1}^{N} (-c_n x_n + p_n z_n) - c_0 x_0 - dy - C\delta \\
\text{s.t.} \quad & (I_n - D_n)x_n - z_n = 0 \quad \left.\begin{aligned} \\ z_n \leq f_n \end{aligned}\right\} n=1,\ldots,N \\
& \sum_{n=1}^{N} A_n x_n \leq a \\
& \sum_{n=1}^{N} B_n x_n - (I - D_0)x_0 - y \leq 0 \\
& x_0 - W\delta \leq 0 \\
& x_n, z_n \ (n=1,\ldots,N), \ x_0, y \geq 0 \\
& \delta \ \text{0-1 vector}
\end{aligned}
$$

$$\text{(E.1)}$$

Recall from chapter three that, among other assumptions, we assume c_0, d, C > 0 and B_n (n=1,...,N), $D_0 \geq 0$.

Before clarifying the link between problem (6.1) and problem (E.1), we investigate optimal solutions of problem (E.1).

Lemma E.1:

Consider an optimal solution to problem (E.1) denoted by x_0^{opt}, y^{opt}, δ^{opt}, x_n^{opt} (n=1,...,N), z_n^{opt} (n=1,...,N).

Assume that we have

$$\delta^{opt}(m) = 0 \Rightarrow (\sum_{n=1}^{N} B_n x_n^{opt} + D_0 x_0^{opt})(m) > 0, \quad m=1,\ldots,M \qquad (E.2)$$

Then

$$\delta^{opt}(m) = 1 \Rightarrow x_0^{opt}(m) > 0, \quad y^{opt}(m) = 0 \qquad (E.3\text{-}a)$$

$$\delta^{opt}(m) = 0 \Rightarrow x_0^{opt}(m) = 0, \quad y^{opt}(m) > 0 \qquad (E.3\text{-}b)$$

and

$$\sum_{n=1}^{N} B_n x_n^{opt} - (I - D_0)x_0^{opt} - y^{opt} = 0 \qquad (E.4)$$

Proof:

If $\delta^{opt}(m) = 0$, then $x_0^{opt}(m) = 0$ because of the constraints $x_0^{opt}(m) - W\delta^{opt}(m) \leq 0$, and thus $y^{opt}(m) > 0$ because of assumption (E.2).

If $\delta^{opt}(m) = 1$, then $x_0^{opt}(m) > 0$ because of C(m) > 0.

Now we are going to prove that $y^{opt}(m) = 0$ if $\delta^{opt}(m) = 1$. Consider problem (E.1) with δ and x_n held fixed: $\delta = \delta^{opt}$ and $x_n = x_n^{opt}$ (n=1,...,N). It follows that $z_n = (I_n - D_n)x_n^{opt} = z_n^{opt}$ (n=1,...,N), so that we have at hand a continuous LP problem with x_0, y as the only variables. For any optimal solution $(\hat{x}_0, \hat{y})$ it holds that $(x_1^{opt}, z_1^{opt},\ldots,x_N^{opt}, z_N^{opt}, \hat{x}_0, \hat{y}, \delta^{opt})$ is optimal to the original problem (E.1). As a result $\hat{x}_0(m) > 0$ if $\delta^{opt}(m) = 1$, and $\hat{x}_0(m) = 0$ if $\delta^{opt}(m) = 0$, i.e. we know in advance which elements of x_0 are positive and which elements are zero in an optimal situation. Therefore the above mentioned continuous LP problem can be written in the following form:

Minimize $\quad \tilde{c}_0 \tilde{x}_0 + \tilde{d}\tilde{y} + \tilde{\tilde{d}}\tilde{\tilde{y}}$

s.t. $\quad (I - D_0) \begin{bmatrix} \tilde{x}_0 \\ 0 \end{bmatrix} + \begin{bmatrix} \tilde{y} \\ 0 \end{bmatrix} + \begin{bmatrix} 0 \\ \tilde{\tilde{y}} \end{bmatrix} - \begin{bmatrix} \tilde{sb} \\ \tilde{\tilde{sb}} \end{bmatrix} = \sum_{n=1}^{N} B_n x_n^{opt}$

$$\tilde{x}_0, \; \tilde{y}, \; \tilde{\tilde{y}}, \; \tilde{sb}, \; \tilde{\tilde{sb}} \geqslant 0 \qquad\qquad (E.5)$$

Here $\tilde{sb}$ and $\tilde{\tilde{sb}}$ are slack variables. Note that the constant terms
$\sum_{n=1}^{N} (-c_n x_n^{opt} + p_n z_n^{opt}) - C\delta^{opt}$ and the redundant constraints $x_0 \leqslant W\delta^{opt}$
are omitted in formulation (E.5).

Basic feasible solutions to the LP problem (E.5) have at most M positive elements. Optimal solutions must have $\tilde{x}_0 > 0$, $\tilde{\tilde{y}} > 0$ and this yields already M positive elements. Hence optimal basic solutions have exactly M positive elements, viz. the elements of $\tilde{x}_0$ and $\tilde{\tilde{y}}$. As a consequence the $\tilde{y}$-part, $\tilde{sb}$-part and $\tilde{\tilde{sb}}$-part must be equal to zero. Now suppose that no unbounded solution exists that attains the finite optimal solution value. Then each optimal solution to (E.5) can be written as a convex combination of the optimal basic solutions, so that $\tilde{y}=0$, $\tilde{sb}=0$, $\tilde{\tilde{sb}}=0$.
Suppose an extreme ray, say $(\tilde{x}_0^r, \tilde{y}^r, \tilde{\tilde{y}}^r, \tilde{sb}^r, \tilde{\tilde{sb}}^r)$, exists along which the optimal solution value is maintained. Then $\tilde{x}_0^r$, $\tilde{y}^r$ and $\tilde{\tilde{y}}^r$ are identically zero, because $\tilde{c}, \tilde{d}, \tilde{\tilde{d}} > 0$. If some element of $\tilde{sb}^r$ or $\tilde{\tilde{sb}}^r$ tends to $+\infty$, then the corresponding element of $\tilde{x}_0^r$, $\tilde{\tilde{y}}^r$ tends to $+\infty$ as well. But this contradicts the requirements $\tilde{x}_0^r = 0$, $\tilde{\tilde{y}}^r = 0$. Hence extreme rays of the feasible region of (E.5) can be neglected.

The conclusion is that optimal solutions to (E.5) must have $\tilde{y} = 0$, $\tilde{sb} = 0$, $\tilde{\tilde{sb}} = 0$, which, in turn, proves (E.3-b) and (E.4) respectively.

$\hfill$ (End of proof)

Now we can prove an important theorem concerning problem (E.1). Recall that there are L different CR-types, so there are L common constraints. Furthermore Φ_n denotes the number of product types in division n.

<u>Theorem E.1:</u>
Let δ^{opt} be part of an optimal solution to problem (E.1). Assume that the continuous LP problem that is obtained by taking δ equal to δ^{opt} has a unique optimal solution, say x_n^{opt}, z_n^{opt} (n=1,...,N), x_0^{opt}, y^{opt}, with

the following two properties:

1. in every division every product is produced;

2. $\delta^{opt}(m) = 0 \Rightarrow (\sum_{n=1}^{N} B_n x_n^{opt} + D_0 x_0^{opt})(m) > 0$, $m=1,\ldots,M$.

For this solution we define μ_n, β_n, SA as follows:

μ_n := number of techniques as applied in division n ($n=1,\ldots,N$);

β_n := number of product types in division n that are sold but below the outside demand level, so $0 \leqslant \beta_n \leqslant \Phi_n$ ($n=1,\ldots,N$);

SA := number of CR-types that are not fully used up, so $0 \leqslant SA \leqslant L$.

Now it holds that:

$$\mu_n - \Phi_n \geqslant 0, \quad n=1,\ldots,N \tag{E.6-a}$$

$$0 \leqslant \sum_{n=1}^{N} ((\mu_n - \Phi_n) + \beta_n \leqslant L - SA \tag{E.6-b}$$

Proof:

From property 1. it follows that for each ϕ ($\phi=1,\ldots,\Phi_n$) at least one ψ exists with $x_{n,\phi}(\psi) > 0$, so that $\mu_n - \Phi_n \geqslant 0$ ($n=1,\ldots,N$). Knowing in advance which elements of x_0 will turn out to be positive (recall Lemma E.1) the continuous LP problem can be rewritten as follows:

$$\text{Maximize} \quad \sum_{n=1}^{N} (c_n x_n + p_n z_n) - \tilde{c}_0 \tilde{x}_0 - \tilde{d}\tilde{y} - \tilde{\tilde{d}}\tilde{\tilde{y}}$$

$$\text{s.t.} \quad (I_n - D_n)x_n - z_n = 0$$
$$z_n \leqslant f_n$$
$$\sum_{n=1}^{N} A_n x_n \leqslant a$$
$$\sum_{n=1}^{N} B_n x_n - (I - D_0)\begin{bmatrix}\tilde{x}_0 \\ \hline 0\end{bmatrix} - \begin{bmatrix}\tilde{y} \\ \hline 0\end{bmatrix} - \begin{bmatrix}0 \\ \hline \tilde{\tilde{y}}\end{bmatrix} \leqslant 0$$
$$x_n, z_n \ (n=1,\ldots,N), \tilde{x}_0, \tilde{y}, \tilde{\tilde{y}} \geqslant 0 \tag{E.7}$$

The optimum of this LP problem is unique and coincides with one of the basic feasible solutions. Hence the optimal solution has

$\sum_{n=1}^{N} 2\Phi_n + L + M - \Theta$ positive elements, where Θ denotes the number of basic zeros of the optimal basic solution.

On the other hand:

x_n yields μ_n positive elements $(n=1,\ldots,N)$;

z_n and the slack variables associated to $z_n \leq f_n$ yield $\Phi_n + \beta_n$ positive elements $(n=1,\ldots,N)$;

the slack variables associated to $\sum_{n=1}^{N} A_n x_n \leq a$ yield SA positive elements;

we are considering an optimal solution so furthermore only $\tilde{x}_0 > 0$ and $\tilde{y} > 0$, which yields M positive elements (recall Lemma E.1). The optimal basic solution thus possesses $\sum_{n=1}^{N} (\mu_n + \Phi_n + \beta_n) + SA + M$ positive elements and this number must be equal to $\sum_{n=1}^{N} 2\Phi_n + L + M - \Theta$. It follows that

$$\sum_{n=1}^{N} ((\mu_n - \Phi_n) + \beta_n) = L - SA - \Theta.$$

Because $\mu_n - \Phi_n \geq 0$, $\beta_n \geq 0$, $\Theta \geq 0$, the conclusion is that

$$0 \leq \sum_{n=1}^{N} ((\mu_n - \Phi_n) + \beta_n) \leq L - SA$$

(End of proof)

We return to the original MIP problem (6.1) and clarify the link with problem (E.1).

From the beginning of this appendix it follows that every feasible and thus every optimal solution to (6.1) can be transformed into a feasible solution of (E.1) without changing the solution value. Reversely, let x_n^{opt}, z_n^{opt} $(n=1,\ldots,N)$, x_0^{opt}, y^{opt}, δ^{opt} be optimal to (E.1). Define $(m=1,\ldots,M)$:

$$b_n(m) := \left(\sum_{n=1}^{N} B_n x_n^{opt} \right)(m) \text{ and } y_n(m) := 0 \text{ if } \delta^{opt}(m) = 1;$$

$$b_n(m) := 0 \text{ and } y_n(m) := \left(\sum_{n=1}^{N} B_n x_n^{opt} \right)(m) \text{ if } \delta^{opt}(m) = 0;$$

$$y_0 := y - \sum_{n=1}^{N} y_n;$$

$$b_0 := \sum_{n=1}^{N} b_n.$$

Note that some $b_0(m)$ can only be positive if $\delta^{opt}(m) = 1$, so constraint $b_0 - W\delta^{opt} \leqslant 0$ is fulfilled. Together with x_n^{opt}, z_n^{opt} $(n=1,\ldots,N)$, vectors b_n, y_n $(n=1,\ldots,N)$, b_0, y_0 form a feasible solution to problem (6.1) with unchanged solution value. Now it is clear that there is a mutual correspondence between the optimal solutions of (E.1) and (6.1). Therefore the following result, which is similar to Lemma E.1, holds:

<u>Lemma E.2:</u>

Let x_n^{opt}, y_n^{opt}, z_n^{opt}, b_n^{opt} $(n=1,\ldots,N)$, x_0^{opt}, y_0^{opt}, b_0^{opt}, δ^{opt} be optimal to problem (6.1). Assume that condition (E.2) is fulfilled. Then this solution has the following property $(m=1,\ldots,M)$:

$$\delta^{opt}(m) = 1 \Rightarrow x_0^{opt}(m) > 0, \; y_n^{opt}(m) = 0, \; n=1,\ldots,N, \; y_0^{opt}(m) = 0; \quad \text{(E.8-a)}$$

$$\delta^{opt}(m) = 0 \Rightarrow x_0^{opt}(m) = 0, \; y_n^{opt}(m) \geqslant 0, \; n=1,\ldots,N, \; y_0^{opt}(m) \geqslant 0. \quad \text{(E.8-b)}$$

We see that overall solutions, i.e. optimal solutions to problem (6.1), capture 'pure' TS alternatives: if some TS-type is produced internally, no additional amounts of this TS-type are bought from outside the firm; if some TS-type is bought externally, there is no internal production of this TS-type. The δ-part of an overall solution expresses which TS-types are entirely produced internally and which TS-types are entirely bought externally.

As a second consequence, Theorem E.1 is not only valid for problem (E.1) but also for problem (6.1). Together with Lemma E.2 this result proves Theorem 6.2. Finally, Theorem 6.1 is just a special case of Theorem 6.2, namely the case L = 0.

APPENDIX F: appendix to CHAPTER SEVEN

This appendix contains a proof of Theorem 7.1 as presented in section 7.3.2. Consider the divisional problem

$$\text{Maximize} \qquad - \tilde{c}_n x_n - \tilde{\tilde{d}} y_n + p_n z_n$$

$$\text{s.t.} \qquad A_n x_n \qquad\qquad \leq \bar{a}_n^k$$

$$\tilde{B}_n x_n - \tilde{y}_n \qquad \leq \tilde{b}_n^k$$

$$(I_n - D_n) x_n \qquad - \quad z_n = 0$$

$$z_n \leq f_n$$

$$x_n, y_n, z_n \geq 0 \tag{7.3}$$

It is assumed that $\bar{a}_n^k > 0$, $f_n > 0$. Furthermore $\tilde{b}_n^k > 0$ as $\tilde{b}_n^k$ contains the TS-types that are actually supplied to the division. The remaining TS-types are not internally available in the current planning session. If the division requires them, they must entirely be bought externally. The associated costs are included in the objective function. For this reason, we have written $\tilde{c}_n$ instead of c_n. Now we present a theorem concerning optimal basic solutions to (7.3). Recall that Φ_n denotes the number of market products in division n, L is the dimension of $\bar{a}_n^k$ and M_n^k is the dimension of $\tilde{b}_n^k$.

<u>Theorem 7.1</u>

Consider an optimal basic solution to problem (7.3) with $\bar{a}_n^k > 0$, $\tilde{b}_n^k > 0$, $f_n > 0$. For this solution:

1. we assume that for each product at least one technique is applied;
2. we define μ_n^k, β_n^k, SA_n^k, SB_n^k, σ_n^k and θ_n^k as follows:

μ_n^k := the number of applied techniques, so $\mu_n^k \geq \Phi_n$;

β_n^k := the number of product types that are sold but below the outside demand level, so $0 \leq \beta_n^k \leq \Phi_n$;

SA_n^k := the number of CR-types that are not fully used up, so $0 \leq SA_n^k \leq L$;

M_n^k := the dimension of $\tilde{b}_n^k$, i.e. the number of TS-types that are internally supplied to division n;

SB_n^k := the number of TS-types that are internally supplied but not fully used up, so $0 \leqslant SB_n^k \leqslant M_n^k$;

σ_n^k := the number of TS-types that are internally supplied and also bought from outside the firm, so $0 \leqslant \sigma_n^k \leqslant M_n^k$;

θ_n^k := the number of basic zeros.

Now it holds that:

$$\sigma_n^k + SB_n^k \leqslant M_n^k, \tag{7.4-a}$$

$$(\mu_n^k - \Phi_n) + \beta_n^k + \sigma_n^k = (L - SA_n^k) + (M_n^k - SB_n^k) - \theta_n^k \tag{7.4-b}$$

Proof:

We write the constraints of (7.3) in equality formulation by adding slack variables, thus obtaining:

$$
\begin{aligned}
A_n x_n \quad &+ sa_n &&= \bar{a}_n^k \\
\tilde{B}_n x_n - \tilde{y}_n \quad &+ sb_n &&= \tilde{b}_n^k \\
(I_n - D_n)x_n \quad - z_n \quad &&&= 0 \\
z_n \quad &+ sf_n &&= f_n
\end{aligned}
$$

We consider an optimal situation, so for all m we have $sb_n(m) \cdot y_n(m) = 0$ (externally bought TS are fully used up). As a result, $\sigma_n^k + SB_n^k \leqslant M_n^k$, which proves formula (7.4-a).

Now we are going to count the number of positive elements in the optimal basic solution at hand.

Vector x_n delivers μ_n positive elements. As each product is produced, $\mu_n^k > \Phi_n$.

As $f_n > 0$, vectors z_n and sf_n deliver $\alpha_n^k + \beta_n^k + \beta_n^k + \gamma_n^k = \Phi_n + \beta_n^k$ positive elements. Here α_n^k denotes the number of product types that are maximally sold and γ_n^k denotes the number of product types that are not sold at all, so that $\alpha_n^k + \beta_n^k + \gamma_n^k = \Phi_n$.

By definition, vectors sa_n, sb_n and $\tilde{y}_n$ deliver SA_n^k, SB_n^k and σ_n^k positive elements, respectively.

Hence, the total number of positive elements in the basic optimal solution at hand is given by the expression:

$$\mu_n^k + \Phi_n + \beta_n^k + SA_n^k + SB_n^k + \sigma_n^k \tag{F.1}$$

On the other hand, problem (7.3) has $L + M_n^k + 2\Phi_n$ rows, so our basic optimal solution has $L + M_n^k + 2\Phi_n - \theta_n^k$ positive elements. Combining this with (F.1) yields the following relationship

$$(\mu_n^k - \Phi_n) + \beta_n^k + \sigma_n^k = (L - SA_n^k) + (M_n^k - SB_n^k) - \theta_n^k$$

and (7.4-b) is proved. (End of proof)

LIST OF SYMBOLS

This list should be used as follows. First one tries to find the unknown symbol in the list of the chapter in which the unknown symbol was noticed. If the unknown symbol is not listed there it can be found in the list with heading 'General symbols'. In case the unknown symbol was noticed in some appendix, one starts with consulting the list of the chapter associated with this appendix. However, symbols that are only used in one specific appendix are not listed here.

Chapter two

D_{MM}^{flow} commodity flow within TS sector

$D_{M\phi}^{flow}$ commodity flow from TS sector to the sector 'products'

$D_{\phi\phi}^{flow}$ commodity flow within the sector 'products'

D_{MM} matrix of intermediate input coefficients with respect to D_{MM}^{flow}

$D_{M\phi}$ matrix of intermediate input coefficients with respect to $D_{M\phi}^{flow}$

$D_{\phi\phi}$ matrix of intermediate input coefficients with respect to $D_{\phi\phi}^{flow}$

Φ number of product types; index is ϕ

X_ϕ ϕ-th product type

$x(\phi)$ units of produced X_ϕ

Ψ_ϕ number of techniques for product X_ϕ; index is ψ

$x_\phi(\psi)$ units of produced X_ϕ by applying technique ψ

$c_{M+\phi}(\psi)$ per-unit direct cost coefficient associated with $x_\phi(\psi)$

x_ϕ production vector of product X_ϕ; elements $\psi_\phi(\psi)$, $\psi=1,\ldots,\Psi_\phi$

x_{prod} total production vector composed from x_ϕ, $\phi=1,\ldots,\Phi$

c_{prod} row vector associated with x_{prod};
   elements $c_{M+\phi}(\psi)$, $\psi=1,\ldots,\Psi_\phi$, $\phi=1,\ldots,\Phi$

$f(\phi)$ outside demand for product X_ϕ

f vector with elements $f(\phi)$, $\phi=1,\ldots,\Phi$

$z(\phi)$ sales level of product X_ϕ

z vector with elements $z(\phi)$, $\phi=1,\ldots,\Phi$

$p(\phi)$ sales price for product X_ϕ

p row vector with elements $p(\phi)$, $\phi=1,\ldots,\Phi$

I_ϕ 'generalized' identity matrix (cf. section 2.3)

D^* input-output matrix of a cost minimizing, pure technology alternative

c^* row vector containing the per-unit direct cost coefficients of a cost minimizing, pure technology alternative

v^* row vector containing the per-unit redistributed variable costs of a cost minimizing, pure technology alternative

$y(m)$ units of externally bought TS_m

y vector with elements $y(m)$, $m=1,\ldots,M$

$b_0(m)$ net demand for TS_m

b_0 vector with elements $b_0(m)$, $m=1,\ldots,M$

$D_{m\phi}(\psi)$ per-unit requirements for TS_m of product ϕ under technique ψ

Chapter three

C_0 joint costs

C_n finishing costs in division n

Y_n costs of independent action by division n

Z_n minimum of Y_n and $C_0 + C_n$

G_n costs allocated to division n

TOTAL $C_0 + C_1 + \ldots + C_N$

$g(m)$ price to be charged to users of TS_m

g' row vector of per-unit redistributed costs; elements $g(m)$, $m=1,\ldots,M$

G' row vector of redistributed costs

x activity vector

p row vector containing per-unit contributions to profit

A, B	coefficient matrices of certain LP problem
a, b	right-hand side vectors of certain LP problem
$\bar{\pi}$	optimal dual variable associated with constraint $Ax \leqslant a$
OPT	gross profit

Chapter four

x_n	activity vector of division n
p_n	row vector containing per-unit contributions to profit
Q_n, q_n	coefficient matrix and right-hand side vector respectively concerning divisional constraints
A_n, B_n	coefficient matrices concerning common constraints
a, b	right-hand side vectors concerning common constraints
$\hat{a}_n, \bar{b}_n$	allocation of common resources to division n
x_n	optimal x_n as computed by division n
$\bar{x}_n$	optimal x_n as computed by the central unit
S_n	number of extreme points in division n
$\bar{S}_n$	number of extreme points in division n known to the central unit
x_n^i	divisional extreme point, $i=1,\ldots,S_n$
p_n^i	$p_n x_n^i$; profit contribution of extreme point x_n^i
A_n^i	$A_n x_n^i$; CR consumption by extreme point x_n^i
$\bar{\pi}_0$	row vector with tentative prices for common resources
$\hat{x}_n^i$	extreme point reported by division n given price $\bar{\pi}_0$
λ_n^i	relative weight of x_n^i to be determined by the central unit
$\bar{\lambda}_n^i$	optimal λ_n^i in intermediate planning session
$(\lambda_n^i)^{opt}$	optimal λ_n^i at the end of the planning procedure
$\hat{P}_n$	profit as reported by division n
$\bar{P}_n$	profit of division as estimated by the central unit
$\bar{\omega}_n$	net profit contribution of basic revealed extreme points

$P_n(b_n)$ maximal profit of division n given b_n

$\hat{\rho}_n$ per-unit valuation of $\bar{b}_n$ as reported by division n

$(\hat{\rho}_n, \hat{\eta}_n)$ optimal dual extreme point of division n

π_0^{opt} $\bar{\pi}_0$ of the final planning session

a_n^{opt} final CR allocation based on $(\lambda_n^i)^{opt}$, $i=1,\ldots,\bar{S}_n$

Chapter five

DMD   division-oriented mixed decomposition

RMD   resource-oriented mixed decomposition

x_n activity vector of division n

P_n row vector containing per-unit contributions to profit

$Q_n,\ q_n$ coefficients matrix and right-hand side vector respectively concerning divisional constraints

F_n feasible region of division n

$A_n,\ B_n$ coefficient matrices concerning common constraints

$a\ ,\ b$ right-hand side vectors concerning common constraints

$\bar{\pi}_0$ tentative price for common resources

$\bar{b}_2$ tentative allocation of common resources to division 2

S_1 number of extreme points of F_1

S_2 number of dual extreme points of division 2

x_1^i extreme point of division 1, $i=1,\ldots,S_1$

(ρ_2^j, η_2^j) dual extreme point of division 2, $j=1,\ldots,S_2$

FMP   full master problem

FMP-d   dual of FMP

RMP   restricted master problem

RMP-d   dual of RMP

λ^i, P_2, b_2 variables in FMP and RMP

μ^j, π_0, π_1 variables in FMP-d and RMP-d

U_n set of feasible CR allocations for division n

U set of globally feasible allocations

$L(x,\pi)$ Lagrange function; x replaces $x_1,\ldots,x_N$

$(\tilde{x},\tilde{\pi})$ saddle point of $L(x,\pi)$

$P_n(\pi,b_n)$ division profit given price π for (*) resources and allocation b_n of (**) resources

(D) dual problem

(P) primal problem

v dual objective function

w primal objective function

$v(D)$ optimal solution value of (D)

$w(P)$ optimal solution value of (P)

r current planning session

k index for planning sessions up to now, $k=1,\ldots,r$

(D_r) relaxed dual problem

(P_r) relaxed primal problem

v^r optimal solution value of (P_r)

w^r optimal solution value of (D_r)

π^k tentative price for (*) resources in k-th planning session

b_n^k tentative allocation of (**) resources in k-th planning session

$\hat{x}_n^{k+1}$ divisional activity plan given π^k and b_n^k

$\hat{\rho}_n^{k+1}$ per-unit valuation of b_n^k by division n given π^k and b_n^k

Δ_a^k, P_{sum}^k cf. (5.24)

ε desired accuracy

λ^k weighting factor

$\bar{\lambda}^k$ optimal λ^k computed by the central unit

$\bar{x}_n$ x_n computed by the central unit; cf. (5.32)

$\bar{a}_n^r, \bar{b}_n^r$ cf. (5.34)

Chapter six

x_n^{opt} — x_n-part of overall solution

a_n^{opt} — $A_n x_n^{opt}$

$\hat{\pi}_n^{opt}$ — per-unit valuation of a_n^{opt}

$V(a)$ — $\hat{\pi}_1^{opt} a_1^{opt} + \ldots + \hat{\pi}_N a_N^{opt}$

g^{opt} — row vector of per-unit redistributed TS costs

Chapter seven

$\bar{a}_n^k$ — CR allocation to division n in k-th planning session

$\bar{b}_n^k$ — internal TS allocation to division n in k-th planning session

$\tilde{b}_n^k$ — cf. introduction to problem (7.3)

$\bar{P}_n^k$ — divisional profit estimated by the central unit in k-th planning session

$\hat{P}_n^k$ — divisional profit given $\bar{a}_n^k$ and $\bar{b}_n^k$

$\hat{\pi}_n^k$ — per-unit valuation of $\bar{a}_n^k$

$\hat{\rho}_n^k$ — per-unit valuation of $\bar{b}_n^k$

$\hat{\eta}_n^k$ — per-unit valuation of f_n given $\bar{a}_n^k$, $\bar{b}_n^k$

V — TS production domain

$P_n(a_n, b_n)$ — divisional profit given a_n and b_n

$g^k(m)$ — price for TS_m in k-th planning session

g^k — row vector; elements $g^k(m)$, $m=1,\ldots,M$

g^{opt} — g^k in the final planning session

a_n^{opt} $\bar{a}_n^k$ in the final planning session

b_n^{opt} $\bar{b}_n^k$ in the final planning session

P_n^{opt} divisional profit given a_n^{opt} and b_n^{opt}

$\hat{\pi}_n^{opt}$ final valuation of allocated CR by division n

$V(a)$ $\hat{\pi}_1^{opt} a_1^{opt} + \ldots + \hat{\pi}_N^{opt} \hat{a}_N^{opt}$

General symbols

LP	linear programming
MIP	mixed integer programming
L	number of CR-types; index is l
M	number of TS-types; index is m
N	number of product divisions; index is subscript n
TS	technical services
TS_m	m-th TS-type, m=1,...,M
CR	common resources
GS	general services
H	common costs
h	fraction of a shadow price; used for common cost allocation
a	CR capacity
A_n	coefficient matrix with respect to CR consumption
a_n	CR allocation to division n
$x_0(m)$	units of internally produced TS_m
x_0	internal-TS production vector with elements $x_0(m)$, m=1,...,M
$diag[x_0]$	diagonal matrix; $diag[x_0]_{mm} := x_0(m)$
$c_0(m)$	per-unit direct costs of producing TS_m internally
c_0	row vector with elements $c_0(m)$, m=1,...,M
$C(m)$	fixed costs of producing TS_m internally
C	row vector with elements $C(m)$, m=1,...,M

$\delta(m)$	0-1 variable associated with making or buying TS_m
δ	vector with elements $\delta(m)$, $m=1,\ldots,M$
W	large positive constant representing maximum capacity of internal TS production
$d(m)$	external price for TS_m
d	row vector with elements $d(m)$, $m=1,\ldots,M$
$y_n(m)$	units of externally bought TS_m by division n
y_n	vector with elements $y_n(m)$, $m=1,\ldots,M$
$y_0(m)$	units of externally bought TS_m used in the internal production of other TS-types
y_0	vector with elements $y_0(m)$, $m=1,\ldots,M$
$b_n(m)$	units of internally produced TS_m as supplied to division n
b_n	vector of internal-TS supply to division n; elements $b_n(m)$, $m=1,\ldots,M$
$b_0(m)$	units of internally produced TS_m supplied to the divisions
b_0	vector of internal-TS supply; elements $b_0(m)$, $m=1,\ldots,M$
B_n	coefficient matrix with respect to TS consumption
Φ_n	number of product types in division n; index is ϕ
$X_{n,\phi}$	ϕ-th product type in division n
$\Psi_{n,\phi}$	number of techniques for product type $X_{n,\phi}$; index is ψ
$x_{n,\phi}(\psi)$	units of produced $X_{n,\phi}$ by using technique ψ
$x_{n,\phi}$	production vector of product type $X_{n,\phi}$; elements $x_{n,\phi}(\psi)$, $\psi=1,\ldots,\Psi_{n,\phi}$
x_n	production vector of division n composed from $x_{n,\phi}$, $\phi=1,\ldots,\Phi_n$
c_n	row vector containing all per-unit direct cost coefficients associated with x_n
f_n	outside demand vector for product types $X_{n,\phi}$, $\phi=1,\ldots,\Phi_n$
p_n	row vector containing the sales prices of $X_{n,\phi}$, $\phi=1,\ldots,\Phi_n$
z_n	outside supply vector for product types $X_{n,\phi}$, $\phi=1,\ldots,\Phi_n$
$D_{n,\phi}$	matrix composed from the $\Psi_{n,\phi}$ columns of intermediate input coefficients for product type $X_{n,\phi}$
D_n	matrix composed from $D_{n,\phi}$, $\phi=1,\ldots,\Phi_n$
I_n	'generalized' identity matrix (cf. section 3.5)

π_n dual variable associated with CR constraints

ρ_n dual variable associated with TS constraints

k superscript referring to a specific planning session

μ_n number of applied techniques in division n

μ_n^k μ_n in the k-th planning session

β_n number of product types that are sold but not maximally

β_n^k β_n in the k-th planning session

SA number of CR types not fully used up

SA_n^k SA in division in k-th planning session

REFERENCES

Anthony, R.N. and J. Dearden (1976), Management control systems: text and cases, Richard D. Irwin Inc., Homewood, Illinois.

Atkins, D.R. (1973), Managerial decentralization and decomposition in mathematical programming, Operational Research Quarterly, 25, no. 4, pp. 615-624.

Atkins, D.R. (1979), Decentralization by joint price and budget controls: the problem and an important special case, Working paper, University of British Columbia.

Baker, K.R. and R.E. Taylor (1979), A linear programming framework for cost allocation and external acquisition when reciprocal services exist, The Accounting Review, 54, no. 4, October 1979, pp. 784-790.

Balanchandran, B.V. and R.T.S. Ramakrishnan (1981), Joint cost allocation: a unified approach, The Accounting Review, 56, no. 1, pp. 85-96.

Baumol, W.J. and T. Fabian (1964), Decomposition, pricing for decentralization and external economies. Management Science, 11, no. 1, pp. 1-32.

Baumol, W.J. (1977), Economic theory and operations analysis, fourth edition, Prentice-hall International, London.

Benders, J.F. (1962), Partitioning procedures for solving mixed-variables programming problems, Numerische Mathematik, 4, pp. 238-252.

Berman, A. and R.J. Plemmons (1979), Non-negative matrices in the mathematical sciences, Academic Press, New York.

Biddle, G.C. and R. Steinberg (1985), Common cost allocation in the firm, in H.P. Young (ed.): Cost allocation: methods, principles, applications, North-Holland, Amsterdam, New York, Oxford, pp. 31-54.

Burton, R.M. and B. Obel (1980), The efficiency of the price, budget, and mixed approaches under varying a-priori information levels for decentralized planning, Management Science, 26, no. 4, April 1980, pp. 401-416.

Capettini, R. and G.L. Salamon (1977), Internal vs. external acquisition of services when reciprocal services exist, The Accounting Review, 52, no. 3, July 1977, pp. 690-696.

Cohen, S.I. and M. Loeb (1982), Public goods, common inputs, and the efficiency of full allocations, The Accounting Review, 57, no. 2, pp. 336-347.

Dantzig, G.B. (1963), Linear programming and extensions, Princeton University Press, Princeton, New Jersey.

Demski, J.S. and D.M. Kreps (1982), Models in managerial accounting, Journal of Accounting Research, 20, Supplement 1982, pp. 117-148.

Dessler, G.D. (1982), Management fundamentals: modern principles & practices, Reston Publishing Company, Reston, Virginia.

Dirickx, Y.M.I. and L.P. Jennergren (1979), Systems analysis by multi-level methods: with applications to economics and management, Wiley, New York.

Dopuch, N., J.G. Birnberg and J.S. Demski (1982), Cost accounting: accounting data for management decisions, 3rd edition, Harcourt, Brace, Jovanovich.

Findeisen, W., F.N. Bailey, M. Brdyś, K. Malinowski, P. Tatjewski, and A. Woźniak (1980), Control and coordination in hierarchical systems, Wiley, New York.

Frauendorfer, K. (1984), Decentralized planning in hierarchical organizations, unpublished Ph.D. dissertation, Linz, Austria.

Geoffrion, A.M. (1970-a), Primal resource-directive approaches for optimizing nonlinear decomposable systems, Operations Research, May-June 1970.

Geoffrion, A.M. (1970-b), Elements of large-scale mathematical programming I and II, Management Science, 16, no. 11, pp. 652-691.

Himmelblau, D.M. (ed.) (1972), Decomposition of large-scale problems, North-Holland, Amsterdam.

Hirschleifer, J. (1956), On the economics of transfer pricing, Journal of Business, 29, pp. 172-184.

Horngren, C.T. (1982), Cost accounting: a managerial emphasis, Prentice Hall, Englewood Cliffs N.J.

Hughes, J.S. and J.H. Scheiner (1980), Efficiency properties of mutually satisfactory cost allocations, The Accounting Review, 55, no. 1, pp. 85-95.

Jennergren, L.P. (1976), The multilevel approach: a systems analysis methodology, Journal of Systems Engineering, 4, no. 2, pp. 97-106.

Jennergren, L.P. (1980), Decentralization in organizations. In W. Starbuck and P. Nystrom (eds.), Handbook of organizational design, Oxford University Press, Oxford.

Johansen, L. (1978), Lectures on macro economic planning, part 2, centralization, decentralization, planning under uncertainty, North-Holland, Amsterdam, New York, Oxford.

Kaplan, R.S. and G.L. Thompson (1971), Overhead allocation via mathematical programming models, The Accounting Review, 46, April 1971, pp. 352-364.

Kaplan, R.S. (1973), Variable and self-service costs in reciprocal allocation models, The Accounting Review, October 1973, pp. 738-748.

Kaplan, R.S. (1982), Advanced management accounting, Prentice Hall, Englewood Cliffs N.J.

Knudsen, N.C. (1973), Production and cost models of a multi-product firm: a mathematical programming approach, Odense University Studies in History and Social Sciences, 15, Odense University Press, Odense, Denmark.

Lasdon, L.S. (1970), Optimization theory for large systems, Collier-MacMillan, London.

Leontief, W.W. (1936), Quantitative input-output relations in the economic system of the United States, The Review of Economics and Statistics, August 1936.

Livingstone, J.L. (1969), Input-output analysis for cost accounting, planning and control, The Accounting Review, 44, pp. 48-64.

Louderback, J.G. (1976), Another approach to allocating joint costs: a comment, The Accounting Review, 51, no. 3, July 1976, pp. 683-685.

Luna, H.P.L. (1984), A survey on informational decentralization and mathematical programming decomposition, in R.W. Cottle, M.L. Kelmanson and B. Korte (eds.): Mathematical programming, Elsevier Science Publishers B.V., North-Holland.

Manes, R.P., S.H. Park and R. Jensen (1982), Relevant costs of intermediate goods and services, The Accounting Review, 57, no. 3, pp. 594-606.

Meijboom, B.R. (1985), Horizontal mixed decomposition, prize-winning paper at EURO VII, Bologna, 17-19 June 1985; European Journal of Operational Research, 27, no. 1, September 1986.

Meijboom, B.R. (1986), A two-level planning procedure with respect to make-or-buy decisions, including cost allocations, European Journal of Operational Research, 23, pp. 301-309.

Mesarović, M.D., D. Macko and Y. Takahara (1970), Theory of hierarchical, multilevel systems, Academic Press, New York and London.

Molina, F.W. (1979), A survey of resource directive decomposition in mathematical programming, Computing Surveys, 11, no. 2, June 1979.

Moriarity, S. (1975), Another approach to allocating joint costs, The Accounting Review, 50, October 1975, pp. 791-795.

Moriarity, S. (1976), Another approach to allocating joint costs: a reply, The Accounting Review, 51, no. 3, July 1976, pp. 686-687.

Moriarity, S. (ed.) (1981), Joint cost allocations, Proceedings of the University of Oklahoma Conference on cost allocations.

Naylor, T.H. and J.M. Vernon (1969), Micro economics and decision models of the firm, Harcourt, Brace & World, New York.

Obel, B. (1978), An note on mixed procedures for decomposing linear programming problems, Mathematische Operationsforschung und Statistik, Series Optimization, 9, no. 4, pp. 537-544.

Obel, B. (1981), Issues of organizational design: mathematical programming view of organizations, Pergamon Press, Oxford.

Ruefli, T.W. (1974), Analytical models of resource allocation in hierarchical multi-level systems, Socio-Econ. Planning Science, 8, pp. 353-363.

Samuelson, P.A. (1951), Abstract of a theorem, concerning substitutability in open Leontief models, in: T.C. Koopmans (ed.): Activity analysis of production and allocation, proceedings of a conference, Wiley, New York.

Shapiro, J.F. and D.E. White (1982), A hybrid decomposition method for integrating coal supply and demand models, Operations Research, _30_, no. 5, September-October 1982.

Smits, H.A. and P.A. Verheyen (1976), The development of a budgeting model. In C.B. Tilanus (ed.): Quantitative methods in budgeting, Nijhoff, Leiden.

Ten Kate, A. (1972), Decomposition of linear programs by direct distribution, Econometrica, _40_, pp. 883-898.

Thomas, A.L. (1977), A behavioral analysis of joint cost allocation and transfer pricing, Arthur Andersen & Co. Lectures Series.

Verheyen, P.A. (1965), Input-output analysis and the firm, inaugural speech Tilburg University, N.V. Uitgeverij Winants, Heerlen, The Netherlands (in Dutch).

Young, H.P. (ed.) (1985), Cost allocation: methods, principles, applications, North-Holland, Amsterdam, New York, Oxford.

Zangwill, W.I. (1969), Nonlinear programming: a unified approach, Prentice Hall, Englewood Cliffs N.J.

Zimmerman, J.L. (1979), The costs and benefits of cost allocations, The Accounting Review, _54_, no. 3, pp. 504-521.

Vol. 184: R. E. Burkard and U. Derigs, Assignment and Matching Problems: Solution Methods with FORTRAN-Programs. VIII, 148 pages. 1980.

Vol. 185: C. C. von Weizsäcker, Barriers to Entry. VI, 220 pages. 1980.

Vol. 186: Ch.-L. Hwang and K. Yoon, Multiple Attribute Decision Making – Methods and Applications. A State-of-the-Art-Survey. XI, 259 pages. 1981.

Vol. 187: W. Hock, K. Schittkowski, Test Examples for Nonlinear Programming Codes. V. 178 pages. 1981.

Vol. 188: D. Bös, Economic Theory of Public Enterprise. VII, 142 pages. 1981.

Vol. 189: A. P. Lüthi, Messung wirtschaftlicher Ungleichheit. IX, 287 pages. 1981.

Vol. 190: J. N. Morse, Organizations: Multiple Agents with Multiple Criteria. Proceedings, 1980. VI, 509 pages. 1981.

Vol. 191: H. R. Sneessens, Theory and Estimation of Macroeconomic Rationing Models. VII, 138 pages. 1981.

Vol. 192: H. J. Bierens: Robust Methods and Asymptotic Theory in Nonlinear Econometrics. IX, 198 pages. 1981.

Vol. 193: J. K. Sengupta, Optimal Decisions under Uncertainty. VII, 156 pages. 1981.

Vol. 194: R. W. Shephard, Cost and Production Functions. XI, 104 pages. 1981.

Vol. 195: H. W. Ursprung, Die elementare Katastrophentheorie. Eine Darstellung aus der Sicht der Ökonomie. VII, 332 pages. 1982.

Vol. 196: M. Nermuth, Information Structures in Economics. VIII, 236 pages. 1982.

Vol. 197: Integer Programming and Related Areas. A Classified Bibliography. 1978 – 1981. Edited by R. von Randow. XIV, 338 pages. 1982.

Vol. 198: P. Zweifel, Ein ökonomisches Modell des Arztverhaltens. XIX, 392 Seiten. 1982.

Vol. 199: Evaluating Mathematical Programming Techniques. Proceedings, 1981. Edited by J.M. Mulvey. XI, 379 pages. 1982.

Vol. 200: The Resource Sector in an Open Economy. Edited by H. Siebert. IX, 161 pages. 1984.

Vol. 201: P. M. C. de Boer, Price Effects in Input-Output-Relations: A Theoretical and Empirical Study for the Netherlands 1949–1967. X, 140 pages. 1982.

Vol. 202: U. Witt, J. Perske, SMS – A Program Package for Simulation and Gaming of Stochastic Market Processes and Learning Behavior. VII, 266 pages. 1982.

Vol. 203: Compilation of Input-Output Tables. Proceedings, 1981. Edited by J. V. Skolka. VII, 307 pages. 1982.

Vol. 204: K. C. Mosler, Entscheidungsregeln bei Risiko: Multivariate stochastische Dominanz. VII, 172 Seiten. 1982.

Vol. 205: R. Ramanathan, Introduction to the Theory of Economic Growth. IX, 347 pages. 1982.

Vol. 206: M. H. Karwan, V. Lotfi, J. Telgen, and S. Zionts, Redundancy in Mathematical Programming. VII, 286 pages. 1983.

Vol. 207: Y. Fujimori, Modern Analysis of Value Theory. X, 165 pages. 1982.

Vol. 208: Econometric Decision Models. Proceedings, 1981. Edited by J. Gruber. VI, 364 pages. 1983.

Vol. 209: Essays and Surveys on Multiple Criteria Decision Making. Proceedings, 1982. Edited by P. Hansen. VII, 441 pages. 1983.

Vol. 210: Technology, Organization and Economic Structure. Edited by R. Sato and M.J. Beckmann. VIII, 195 pages. 1983.

Vol. 211: P. van den Heuvel, The Stability of a Macroeconomic System with Quantity Constraints. VII, 169 pages. 1983.

Vol. 212: R. Sato and T. Nôno, Invariance Principles and the Structure of Technology. V, 94 pages. 1983.

Vol. 213: Aspiration Levels in Bargaining and Economic Decision Making. Proceedings, 1982. Edited by R. Tietz. VIII, 406 pages. 1983.

Vol. 214: M. Faber, H. Niemes und G. Stephan, Entropie, Umweltschutz und Rohstoffverbrauch. IX, 181 Seiten. 1983.

Vol. 215: Semi-Infinite Programming and Applications. Proceedings, 1981. Edited by A. V. Fiacco and K. O. Kortanek. XI, 322 pages. 1983.

Vol. 216: H. H. Müller, Fiscal Policies in a General Equilibrium Model with Persistent Unemployment. VI, 92 pages. 1983.

Vol. 217: Ch. Grootaert, The Relation Between Final Demand and Income Distribution. XIV, 105 pages. 1983.

Vol. 218: P. van Loon, A Dynamic Theory of the Firm: Production, Finance and Investment. VII, 191 pages. 1983.

Vol. 219: E. van Damme, Refinements of the Nash Equilibrium Concept. VI, 151 pages. 1983.

Vol. 220: M. Aoki, Notes on Economic Time Series Analysis: System Theoretic Perspectives. IX, 249 pages. 1983.

Vol. 221: S. Nakamura, An Inter-Industry Translog Model of Prices and Technical Change for the West German Economy. XIV, 290 pages. 1984.

Vol. 222: P. Meier, Energy Systems Analysis for Developing Countries. VI, 344 pages. 1984.

Vol. 223: W. Trockel, Market Demand. VIII, 205 pages. 1984.

Vol. 224: M. Kiy, Ein disaggregiertes Prognosesystem für die Bundesrepublik Deutschland. XVIII, 276 Seiten. 1984.

Vol. 225: T. R. von Ungern-Sternberg, Zur Analyse von Märkten mit unvollständiger Nachfragerinformation. IX, 125 Seiten. 1984

Vol. 226: Selected Topics in Operations Research and Mathematical Economics. Proceedings, 1983. Edited by G. Hammer and D. Pallaschke. IX, 478 pages. 1984.

Vol. 227: Risk and Capital. Proceedings, 1983. Edited by G. Bamberg and K. Spremann. VII, 306 pages. 1984.

Vol. 228: Nonlinear Models of Fluctuating Growth. Proceedings, 1983. Edited by R. M. Goodwin, M. Krüger and A. Vercelli. XVII, 277 pages. 1984.

Vol. 229: Interactive Decision Analysis. Proceedings, 1983. Edited by M. Grauer and A. P. Wierzbicki. VIII, 269 pages. 1984.

Vol. 230: Macro-Economic Planning with Conflicting Goals. Proceedings, 1982. Edited by M. Despontin, P. Nijkamp and J. Spronk. VI, 297 pages. 1984.

Vol. 231: G. F. Newell, The M/M/∞ Service System with Ranked Servers in Heavy Traffic. XI, 126 pages. 1984.

Vol. 232: L. Bauwens, Bayesian Full Information Analysis of Simultaneous Equation Models Using Integration by Monte Carlo. VI, 114 pages. 1984.

Vol. 233: G. Wagenhals, The World Copper Market. XI, 190 pages. 1984.

Vol. 234: B. C. Eaves, A Course in Triangulations for Solving Equations with Deformations. III, 302 pages. 1984.

Vol. 235: Stochastic Models in Reliability Theory. Proceedings, 1984. Edited by S. Osaki and Y. Hatoyama. VII, 212 pages. 1984.

Vol. 236: G. Gandolfo, P.C. Padoan, A Disequilibrium Model of Real and Financial Accumulation in an Open Economy. VI, 172 pages. 1984.

Vol. 237: Misspecification Analysis. Proceedings, 1983. Edited by T. K. Dijkstra. V, 129 pages. 1984.

Vol. 238: W. Domschke, A. Drexl, Location and Layout Planning. IV, 134 pages. 1985.

Vol. 239: Microeconomic Models of Housing Markets. Edited by K. Stahl. VII, 197 pages. 1985.

Vol. 240: Contributions to Operations Research. Proceedings, 1984. Edited by K. Neumann and D. Pallaschke. V, 190 pages. 1985.

Vol. 241: U. Wittmann, Das Konzept rationaler Preiserwartungen. XI, 310 Seiten. 1985.

Vol. 242: Decision Making with Multiple Objectives. Proceedings, 1984. Edited by Y. Y. Haimes and V. Chankong. XI, 571 pages. 1985.

Vol. 243: Integer Programming and Related Areas. A Classified Bibliography 1981–1984. Edited by R. von Randow. XX, 386 pages. 1985.

Vol. 244: Advances in Equilibrium Theory. Proceedings, 1984. Edited by C. D. Aliprantis, O. Burkinshaw and N. J. Rothman. II, 235 pages. 1985.

Vol. 245: J. E. M. Wilhelm, Arbitrage Theory. VII, 114 pages. 1985.

Vol. 246: P. W. Otter, Dynamic Feature Space Modelling, Filtering and Self-Tuning Control of Stochastic Systems. XIV, 177 pages. 1985.

Vol. 247: Optimization and Discrete Choice in Urban Systems. Proceedings, 1983. Edited by B. G. Hutchinson, P. Nijkamp and M. Batty. VI, 371 pages. 1985.

Vol. 248: Plural Rationality and Interactive Decision Processes. Proceedings, 1984. Edited by M. Grauer, M. Thompson and A. P. Wierzbicki. VI, 354 pages. 1985.

Vol. 249: Spatial Price Equilibrium: Advances in Theory, Computation and Application. Proceedings, 1984. Edited by P. T. Harker. VII, 277 pages. 1985.

Vol. 250: M. Roubens, Ph. Vincke, Preference Modelling. VIII, 94 pages. 1985.

Vol. 251: Input-Output Modeling. Proceedings, 1984. Edited by A. Smyshlyaev. VI, 261 pages. 1985.

Vol. 252: A. Birolini, On the Use of Stochastic Processes in Modeling Reliability Problems. VI, 105 pages. 1985.

Vol. 253: C. Withagen, Economic Theory and International Trade in Natural Exhaustible Resources. VI, 172 pages. 1985.

Vol. 254: S. Müller, Arbitrage Pricing of Contingent Claims. VIII, 151 pages. 1985.

Vol. 255: Nondifferentiable Optimization: Motivations and Applications. Proceedings, 1984. Edited by V. F. Demyanov and D. Pallaschke. VI, 350 pages. 1985.

Vol. 256: Convexity and Duality in Optimization. Proceedings, 1984. Edited by J. Ponstein. V, 142 pages. 1985.

Vol. 257: Dynamics of Macrosystems. Proceedings, 1984. Edited by J.-P. Aubin, D. Saari and K. Sigmund. VI, 280 pages. 1985.

Vol. 258: H. Funke, Eine allgemeine Theorie der Polypol- und Oligopolpreisbildung. III, 237 pages. 1985.

Vol. 259: Infinite Programming. Proceedings, 1984. Edited by E. J. Anderson and A. B. Philpott. XIV, 244 pages. 1985.

Vol. 260: H.-J. Kruse, Degeneracy Graphs and the Neighbourhood Problem. VIII, 128 pages. 1986.

Vol. 261: Th. R. Gulledge, Jr., N. K. Womer, The Economics of Made-to-Order Production. VI, 134 pages. 1986.

Vol. 262: H. U. Buhl, A Neo-Classical Theory of Distribution and Wealth. V, 146 pages. 1986.

Vol. 263: M. Schäfer, Resource Extraction and Market Structure. XI, 154 pages. 1986.

Vol. 264: Models of Economic Dynamics. Proceedings, 1983. Edited by H. F. Sonnenschein. VII, 212 pages. 1986.

Vol. 265: Dynamic Games and Applications in Economics. Edited by T. Başar. IX, 288 pages. 1986.

Vol. 266: Multi-Stage Production Planning and Inventory Control. Edited by S. Axsäter, Ch. Schneeweiss and E. Silver. V, 264 pages. 1986.

Vol. 267: R. Bemelmans, The Capacity Aspect of Inventories. IX, 165 pages. 1986.

Vol. 268: V. Firchau, Information Evaluation in Capital Markets. VII, 103 pages. 1986.

Vol. 269: A. Borglin, H. Keiding, Optimality in Infinite Horizon Economies. VI, 180 pages. 1986.

Vol. 270: Technological Change, Employment and Spatial Dynamics. Proceedings 1985. Edited by P. Nijkamp. VII, 466 pages. 1986.

Vol. 271: C. Hildreth, The Cowles Commission in Chicago, 1939–1955. V, 176 pages. 1986.

Vol. 272: G. Clemenz, Credit Markets with Asymmetric Information. VIII, 212 pages. 1986.

Vol. 273: Large-Scale Modelling and Interactive Decision Analysis. Proceedings, 1985. Edited by G. Fandel, M. Grauer, A. Kurzhanski and A. P. Wierzbicki. VII, 363 pages. 1986.

Vol. 274: W. K. Klein Haneveld, Duality in Stochastic Linear and Dynamic Programming. VII, 295 pages. 1986.

Vol. 275: Competition, Instability, and Nonlinear Cycles. Proceedings, 1985. Edited by W. Semmler. XII, 340 pages. 1986.

Vol. 276: M. R. Baye, D. A. Black, Consumer Behavior, Cost of Living Measures, and the Income Tax. VII, 119 pages. 1986.

Vol. 277: Studies in Austrian Capital Theory, Investment and Time. Edited by M. Faber. VI, 317 pages. 1986.

Vol. 278: W. E. Diewert, The Measurement of the Economic Benefits of Infrastructure Services. V, 202 pages. 1986.

Vol. 279: H.-J. Büttler, G. Frei and B. Schips, Estimation of Disequilibrium Models. VI, 114 pages. 1986.

Vol. 280: H. T. Lau, Combinatorial Heuristic Algorithms with FORTRAN. VII, 126 pages. 1986.

Vol. 281: Ch.-L. Hwang, M.-J. Lin, Group Decision Making under Multiple Criteria. XI, 400 pages. 1987.

Vol. 282: K. Schittkowski, More Test Examples for Nonlinear Programming Codes. V, 261 pages. 1987.

Vol. 283: G. Gabisch, H.-W. Lorenz, Business Cycle Theory. VII, 229 pages. 1987.

Vol. 284: H. Lütkepohl, Forecasting Aggregated Vector ARMA Processes. X, 323 pages. 1987.

Vol. 285: Toward Interactive and Intelligent Decision Support Systems. Volume 1. Proceedings, 1986. Edited by Y. Sawaragi, K. Inoue and H. Nakayama. XII, 445 pages. 1987.

Vol. 286: Toward Interactive and Intelligent Decision Support Systems. Volume 2. Proceedings, 1986. Edited by Y. Sawaragi, K. Inoue and H. Nakayama. XII, 450 pages. 1987.

Vol. 287: Dynamical Systems. Proceedings, 1985. Edited by A. B. Kurzhanski and K. Sigmund. VI, 215 pages. 1987.

Vol. 288: G. D. Rudebusch, The Estimation of Macroeconomic Disequilibrium Models with Regime Classification Information. VII, 128 pages. 1987.

Vol. 289: B. R. Meijboom, Planning in Decentralized Firms. X, 168 pages. 1987.